SMILERS

PART ONE: FROM THE ASHES

SMILERS

PART ONE: FROM THE ASHES

The unique story of an enterprising young company from Kingston upon Hull

DAVID M GARBERA

First published 2009 by

Garbera Enterprise Ltd
141 Fairfax Avenue
Hull
HU5 4QZ
Tel 01482 445357

www.garberaenterprise.co.uk

ISBN 978-0-9561815-0-3

Copyright © David M Garbera 2009

The right of David M Garbera to be identified as the author of this work has been asserted to him in accordance with the Copyright, Designs and Patents Act 1988

All rights reserved. No part of this publication may be reproduced, stored in or introduced into a retrieval system, or transmitted in any form, or by any means (electronic, mechanical, photocopying, recording or otherwise) without the prior written permission of the publisher. Any person who does any unauthorised act in relation to this publication may be liable to criminal prosecution and civil claims for damage.

Printed in England by CPI Antony Rowe, Chippenham, Wiltshire

Dedicated to all 'Smilers' past, present and future

Contents

9	Foreword
11	Preface
13	Birth
16	Trouble At Mill
18	From the Ashes
22	Ready to Launch
26	Road Trip – Venturefest York 2004
29	Blood, Sweat and Tears
35	Adjudication Day
42	KC Stadium
46	"Good aren't they?"
54	Interregnum
60	The City of Steel
68	Interregnum II
73	91 The Strand
80	The Final Countdown
87	The Day of Judgement
99	Going Limited
105	"No-one Ever Remembers Who Came Second"
128	The Final Word
130	Appendices

Foreword

THIS inspiring story takes the reader on a roller coaster ride, taking in the highs and lows of a group of Year 10 secondary school pupils from Hull, who, against all the odds, turned a failing Young Enterprise business into a successful Limited company.

I was delighted when David told me he wanted to pass on his experience of YE, and he has produced a light-hearted but factual account of his journey and achievements. Once I started reading the book I could not put it down. A thoroughly captivating read!

Through their involvement in Young Enterprise, and the experience of taking the business forward as a Limited company, the KH Smilers team developed work place skills in addition to equipping themselves for life in general.

As creative, confident and independent entrepreneurs, the breadth of opportunities which have opened up has placed them streets ahead of their peers, and they continue to be outstanding YE Alumni.

Being the business advisor to KH Smilers has been an extremely rewarding and pleasurable experience. I strongly believe enterprise programmes are an excellent way of bridging the gap between education and business.

In my opinion, anyone involved in Enterprise programmes or the 14-19 Diploma, will find 'Smilers' a unique and invaluable resource.

Vic Golding ACMA,
Managing Director,
Golding Computer Services Ltd, Hull.

Preface

STARTING your own business isn't easy, especially when you are just fifteen years of age with very little time, money and experience. Many young people have the drive, ambition and vision to start a business of their own, with the potential to produce products and services of all types, but have no idea how to begin. Taking part in the Young Enterprise programme gave the 'Smilers' an unparalleled insight in to the world of starting, maintaining and, eventually, liquidating our own business, as well as providing inspiration for us all as potential entrepreneurs of the future. It certainly inspired me.

Running KH Smilers as part of the YE Company Programme changed my life by handing me the springboard from which to make the jump from school project to fully-fledged limited company. YE helped me to unlock a number of key skills, including teamwork, time management, communication techniques, and perhaps most importantly, confidence. Being the managing director also helped me to understand the qualities needed to be a good leader, and how to get the best out of my team, which is very important. Moreover, these skills and qualities have continued to be extremely useful to me as I strive to become a doctor.

Benn, Mike and I have proved that you simply do not have to choose between vocational and academic learning. The two can run hand in hand. Whilst running a successful and profitable business we achieved GCSEs, A-levels and are currently studying for university degrees.

I hope you enjoy reading about the experiences of KH Smilers, and to everyone just starting on their Young Enterprise journey, or contemplating starting their own business, I wish you the very best of luck. The road is long, yet rewarding and incredibly exciting. You never quite know where it is going to take you…

David M Garbera
Hull

February 2009

Birth

THE day had ended. The rain was falling silently on the urban landscape when the sound of a bell screeched through the air. As the noise and mayhem of bodies escaping from the building died down, a small group sat huddled together glancing nervously at each other and talking in whispers. They were waiting. Suddenly, as the veils of darkness began to fill the room, the sound of someone approaching could clearly be heard. Silence descended on the assembled few. They knew WHO was coming but little or nothing of the monumental journey that some of them were about to undertake. A bright light filled the room as the young woman arrived at the door and entered. She smiled knowingly. The fateful hour had finally arrived.

Yes, you've guessed it! The first meeting of the Kelvin Hall School Young Enterprise group had just begun. Alright, maybe it didn't happen quite like that, but it's better than my original start ('Once upon a time there was this school in Hull.....') and you must admit it was a good way of getting your attention. So, now that I've got you where I want you, sit back, get comfy and I will tell you of the wondrous story that is KH Smilers.

It was pitch black that night. The fog was rolling in from the Humber and the sound of a tolling bell could clearly be heard in the distance..........oh, there I go again! Yet more fantasy. But be patient and I promise to do it properly.

Firstly, we need to go back to September 2003 to a school in Kingston upon Hull called Kelvin Hall. This is an 11-16 comprehensive with a population of some 950 students. The Headmaster, until recently, being Mr Martin Doolan.

In previous years Kelvin Hall had not been involved in the Young Enterprise Scheme and business studies was not taught in the school. This was a scary, but strangely exciting scenario for the 18 strong group of Year 10 students (average age 14), who were about to set up their own company, and boldly go where no-one from Kelvin had gone before.

However, they were not alone. Advice and encouragement were readily available from at least two sources. Firstly, from the spiritual Mrs Turnbull, a teacher of RE at the school who became the group's school advisor and secondly, from the experienced Mr Trevor Sellers, Area Quality Manager with HSBC, who became the group's business advisor. With everything in place it was time for the team to make some very important decisions and so, armed with the YE Company Programme pack, the journey began.

THE PRODUCT. After much discussion it was decided that the company would make and sell a range of novelty items. These would be sold at Craft Fayres and similar events. This range would include Christmas cards (and possibly mugs) with smiley faces on. I think you can see where I am going from here, can't you?

THE NAME. You've guessed it - KH Smilers! KH from the school name and Smilers from ....do I need to go on? No. I thought not.

THE DIRECTORS. With eighteen people to choose from,

including Richard Myers and Stu Vernon (more of them later), positions were quickly filled and jobs allocated.

At last KH Smilers was born. Small but perfectly formed it was quickly registered with the YE Company Programme. This meant that shares could be sold and capital raised. Stock (Whacky Test Tubes and Crazy Sand) was ordered and received. There was nothing left to do but to sit back, start trading and watch the money come rolling in. What could possibly be easier?

The spiritual home of the Smilers

Trouble at Mill

IT was now a month later – October 2003 to be exact. The weather in Hull was fine and bright, the 700 year old annual Hull Fair was looming large and I would be 15 years old on October 15. Ah, but I was forgetting, you may be a reader who does not know about Hull Fair or the legendary Carver's patty and chips that can be bought there. For you I suggest a quick 'Googling', but please allow yourself a decent wedge of time to find out more about this great Hull institution, and in my opinion, equally great local culinary delight. But you needn't just take my word for it. I have friends in Liverpool who have recently visited the said attraction, and sampled the aforementioned delight. All will attest to the greatness of both Fair and food. However, that's enough of that for now. Let's move on quickly and get back to the more familiar world of Kelvin Hall School and the YE Company Programme.

Indeed, I would like you to cast your minds back to September and an infant KH Smilers, still in nappies, but ready to enter the world of business and enterprise. If you remember, everything was in place – people, plan and stock. The foundations for success had been laid. Enthusiasm and expectations were high. Surely nothing could go wrong. Oh, yes it could! Oh, no it couldn't! Oh, yes it could! Oh, no...... Stop it now. This isn't a pantomime. Well, not yet anyway. But of course you are absolutely right it could, and it did, go wrong.

Where do I start? Few sales, a lack of confidence, chaotic meetings, resignations, confusion and debt. Lots and lots of debt. And believe it or not, this is when I decided to join the company as Sales Director. Admittedly, I had just stopped taking a mountain of medication for quite a serious medical condition. At the time I thought I was a werewolf, but clearly I'm alright noooooow! Seriously though, I must have been mad to join at this particular juncture. These were very desperate times for KH Smilers. By the end of November the company had hit rock bottom. Production of 'smiley' Christmas cards was abandoned. Sales of Whacky Test Tubes and Crazy Sand were virtually non-existent. The company had fewer than 10 members and falling. Debt had spiralled out of control to £250 and suppliers were demanding to be paid. Decisive action had to be taken and it had to be taken quickly if KH Smilers was going to survive. Fortunately, the Christmas holidays were just round the corner. It's just what we needed - a breathing space. It would give the company time to come up with a new Board of Directors, a new product and a new business plan. Hopefully, this would lead to a happy and prosperous New Year for a revamped and revitalised company. It was time for KH Smilers to grow up!

From the Ashes

A NEW year dawned. A new term began. It was now January 2004 and KH Smilers was ready to take on the world! An EGM (Extra-ordinary General Meeting) was called. Eighteen had now become SIX with only two members surviving from the original company – Richard Myers and Stu Vernon. The remaining four comprised of me, Kathryn Hill, Benn Jessney and Michael Jones. I had joined in October 2003 whilst the others arrived at various times between December 2003 and January 2004. Everyone else had walked away from KH Smilers, a business that appeared to be teetering on the edge of failure and ultimate oblivion. The meeting began.

The team was enthusiastic and motivated. They all wanted KH Smilers to succeed but they also realised they needed more help. Enter Janet Brumby, knight in shining armour, YE Development Manager and erstwhile member of local tribute band, Beautiful Couch. Drawing on her years of experience she provided us with lots of good advice and practical tips that helped to make recovery believable and attainable.

Firstly, a secret ballot was held for positions within the company. After long, nail-biting seconds counting the voting slips the following company structure was implemented:

Managing Director – David Garbera [15 years old]
Marketing Director – Kathryn Hill [15 years old]
Operations Director – Benn Jessney [14 years old]
Sales Director – Michael Jones [14 years old]
Finance Director – Richard Myers [14 years old]
ICT Director – Stu Vernon [14 years old]

It was also agreed that the duties of Personnel and Administration Directors would have to be shared. Flexibility was the key here. After all there were eight jobs but only six in the company. Not really rocket science, eh?

So far, so good. But then that was the easy bit. Being a director is one thing, having a product that will sell and that people want to buy is another. The most crucial decision of all had yet to be taken. This decision would make or break the company.

Fear gripped the boardroom. Brows furrowed and eyes narrowed. Palms sweated and buttocks clenched. The enormity of the situation was weighing heavily on the shoulders of the assembled few. There was silence.

My mind was racing. What could we possibly do? We had already rejected a couple of ideas just before we broke up for the Christmas holiday. Firstly, printing customers' own pictures on to various household objects like mugs and secondly, selling mobile phone car holders (the ban on using mobile phones whilst driving was just coming in) but a supplier couldn't be found. An obvious non-starter! I quickly refocused. There was still silence in the room as the other five minds continued to grapple with the ultimate question. Does God exist? No, not that one stupid! This one. What could KH Smilers sell that people would want to buy?

In the solitude of my own mind, I suddenly felt the pressure of making such an enormous decision drifting away. I was totally calm as my thoughts turned back to a much happier occasion just a few days earlier. I felt a smile develop as I relived the moment. We were in a restaurant – Mustafa's to be exact. Just the four of us - me, my mum, my dad and 'the Grimsta' (a nickname we use for my grandma). The Porterhouse steak that evening was delicious and the chocolate dessert exquisite. I would really like to take the time to describe the dishes to you in much more detail but then you would get bored and I would start to salivate uncontrollably. Not a nice sight. Very messy! Goes back to my werewolf days you know. But as you have probably already guessed the food that evening is not the real point of this story. However, a chance conversation that developed just before I tucked into my starter (for the foodies amongst you it was a scrumptious scampi) sowed the seeds of an idea in my little brain. We were discussing my dad's love of teaching (not!) as he was just about to go back for the spring term. As his eyes began to fill with tears I quickly moved the conversation on to something I knew he really enjoyed – his garden, plants and greenhouses. He brightened up immediately and confided that this was something he would like to do more of when he retired from teaching. This got me thinking. Don't forget I'm still hungry at this point so keeping the brain cells active was quite stressful, but for the sake of KH Smilers I was prepared to soldier on. I muttered something to myself, rather than to my dad, but he replied anyway, "Yeah, I don't see why people wouldn't buy them from you." Eureka! Could this possibly be the idea to save KH Smilers?

At that point my starter arrived and no more was said. The idea lay buried and forgotten until now. But, oh, that starter! It was piping hot and looked so appetising. I opened my mouth and tucked into this wonderful delicacy. Aaah, the taste! Unfortunately, I got no further. The daydream was ending as the real world beckoned. In an instant I was back in the meeting. "We can sell plants!" I shouted triumphantly. There was a sharp intake of breath. I waited for a reaction. Then, as one, fists punched the air and joyous shouts of 'Yes! Yes! Yes! filled the room. The silence had finally broken. We took a moment to let the idea sink in and then eagerly got down to the nitty-gritty of what, where and how? As discussions progressed the team realised that we did indeed have most of the resources to pull this off. It was unanimously agreed. From now on KH Smilers would not be selling novelty items but bedding plants for the coming summer season. Just like the proverbial Phoenix, KH Smilers had risen from the ashes.

Alright, I agree, a bit OTT in parts. But essentially it is the truth and a heck of a lot less boring than 'we decided to grow some plants'!

Inspirational!

Ready to Launch

THE team went home that evening burning with enthusiasm. After all we already had two of the three main resources needed to start up the new business. Firstly, two large greenhouses to grow our plants in and, secondly, expert advice to help us select, nurture and then maintain a selection of appropriate summer bedding plants. Come to think of it though, we did have more than two resources available. I was forgetting about us - the directors. We had a sack full of personal qualities that we could bring to the table, for example the determination to acquire new knowledge and the discipline to learn new skills. More than that, the six of us were absolutely confident, that as individuals, we could run this company and, at the same time, work together as a team to produce an award winning business. If we could get the balance right KH Smilers would be unstoppable.

What we did not have was money - the life blood of any business venture. Actually that's not quite the truth. There was some cash. About £5. And, of course, a mountain of unsold stock (Whacky Test Tubes and Crazy Sand, if you remember). So the procurement of more cash became our first major task. This was urgently needed so that we could pay off the £250 worth of debt incurred by the earlier incarnation of KH Smilers, and to buy in stocks of young bedding plants, horticultural plant containers and compost.

However, within a few days of our EGM money started to flow into the coffers of KH Smilers. At the meeting we had agreed that, in the short term, selling shares in the company would be the easiest way of solving our cash flow problems. As a result the six of us set about cajoling teachers, friends and relatives into buying as many shares as possible, promising handsome dividends in the process. Within a matter of days we had an extra £128.50 in the bank. We were also acutely aware that there was a lot of money tied up in the Whacky Test Tubes and Crazy Sand. Selling this off as quickly as possible became our second major priority – even, dare I say it, at a loss!

By the end of January 2004 we were also taking our first tentative steps into the world of horticulture. Armed with money from the sale of shares and brimming with new found knowledge, the team went in search of inexpensive, but good quality decorative terracotta pots, plants and compost. At B&Q we found all three in abundance. Purchases made, they were expertly bundled into my dad's car and taken back to our new place of work – the 10 X 12ft greenhouse in my back garden. Our first master class into the mystery that is pots and plants was about to begin. After a number of hours and several attempts later, we had produced a pleasing array of colourfully planted decorative pots. More importantly, we had added value. Selling our products and making a profit was now a realistic target. We were equally impressed with our newly acquired practical skills. Our fingers were definitely a little greener!

Then a stroke of good fortune. Janet Brumby, in her role of YE Development Manager, presented us with an offer that we could not refuse. This was an opportunity to launch the company formally and to sell ourselves as a credible business. She handed us an invitation to attend *Venturefest 2004* in the historic city of York. Held at the world famous racecourse this business forum, organised by Yorkshire Forward, would allow us to network with well-established regional companies, as well as to test our skills as salesmen of Whacky Test Tubes (including Crazy Sand) and decorative plant arrangements.

Preparations for our road trip had to be done quickly but professionally. Fortunately, we had already begun to design flyers, posters and order forms. These were quickly finalised and produced. In the process the company adopted the phrase 'Growing a Smile', an inspired contribution by our ICT Director, Stu.

Having just mentioned ICT I must, at this point, give a quick mention to the involvement of a local company that proved to be an invaluable asset to our team – Golding Computer Services. Earlier in the year my mum – General Manager at GCS - had encouraged me to have a chat with MD Vic Golding in the hope that he might be able to offer me a Work Experience place at the end of Year 10. Over a cup of tea I talked to him about my interest in computing/IT and the fact that I had just started a GNVQ in IT at school. I also mentioned KH Smilers and my role as MD within this Young Enterprise Company. This bit of news certainly aroused his curiosity, so we talked a little longer about KH Smilers and the problems it had encountered. However, to cut a long story short, I got my Work Experience place but more importantly, Vic agreed to become our day-to-day business adviser. His knowledge and experience would be extremely useful to a company like KH Smilers, which was just about to take its first steps into the real world of business and enterprise. To have him on board was great news for the team.

Now, back to our preparations for *Venturefest York 2004.* Stu agreed to work on a rolling PowerPoint presentation that would give onlookers details of the new KH Smilers and its living products. The rest of us busied ourselves with designing an eye-catching display and devising other ways of attracting people to our stand. Stock to sell had basically taken care of itself, but we still needed to settle upon our corporate image. With only a few days to go a decision was finally made. As we were all so young we felt that the team not only had to act the part of responsible business men and women but also LOOK the part. Smart black trousers, white shirt, blue tie and black shoes, therefore, became our dress of choice. Only one more decision remained, that is, which Directors of the company would attend the event? Lack of sufficient transport meant that only three of the six-strong team could go. In the end with three of the team having prior commitments it wasn't a problem. Delegates were me, Richard and Stu. KH Smilers was ready to go on the road.

Not quite Route 66 but we were ready to go

Road Trip – Venturefest York 2004

THE first test of KH Smilers as a credible company arrived, in what seemed to be, the blink of an eye. Thursday 5 February 2004. This was the day that we would hit the open road – the A1079 to be precise - to York and *Venturefest 2004*. But one final surprise arrived just the day before we were due to leave. Name badges. No, not the sticky white labels that everyone gets when they go to a meeting and which are simply plonked on your clothing, but proper ones, brand new and professionally made. Our names, position in the company and logo clearly displayed for all to see. Proud? We were over the moon. The KH Smilers package was complete, ready to show the business world that young people from a comprehensive school in Hull could be positive, successful and a credit to the city.

It was 6am when I got up that morning and still pitch black outside. The house was cold as the central heating hadn't come on yet. I was nervous but at the same time very excited. As I showered, brushed my teeth and got dressed I could hear my dad going in and out of the house as he loaded up the car (our ride to York) with display materials, Whacky Test Tubes and the decorative terracotta pots that we had planted up just a few days before. As I came down for my slice of toast he had already finished his breakfast, and was preparing to leave for work at Archbishop

Thurstan School in east Hull (now the Archbishop Sentamu Academy). Briefcase and freshly marked exercise books in hand he wished me good luck and left. Meanwhile my mum was making sure that name badges, business cards and a host of other, small but important details were taken care of. Richard arrived at 6.45am, equally nervous and excited. Without much ado we all got in the car and drove off to pick up Stu.

As we left Stu's house it was exactly 7.00am. Two hours later we arrived at the racecourse. What a horrendous trip! Traffic was unbelievably heavy that particular morning, and so making any sort of progress was incredibly slow, but even worse than that my mum insisted on keeping her window open for the full duration of the journey. Believe you me it was frostbite time. The three of us were blue with the cold and literally frozen to the core. We exited the car like three icepops.

Notwithstanding the cold we quickly bundled all our gear into the waiting lift, and as we disappeared from view my mum wished us luck and drove off back to Hull. We had arrived and were raring to go.

As the lift doors slid open a huge room opened out in front of us and we were hit by the sound of dozens of people preparing for the day. Most exhilarating, although maybe a little bit daunting, as we didn't know anybody at all! The lift was emptied in double quick time as someone told us where we could set up. As a table and display boards were already in place we speedily set about creating a welcoming, colourful and informative trade stand. Marketing material was clearly displayed behind and around the table. Stu set up the projector. It hummed into action. Like magic our faces and company information took it in turn to appear on the screen. On the table Whacky Test Tubes and planted pots were prominently arranged. Finally, to encourage people to come to our stand we put out a bowl of sweets and organised a free raffle (helpful hints from Vic at GCS). The prize would be a large decorative pot that we had planted up and a winner would be independently drawn later in the day. We were ready to rock 'n' roll.

The rest of the day was hugely enjoyable. We all spent so much time networking that we hardly had any time to eat! Before we knew it the raffle (very successful) had been drawn; we had been presented with a commemorative plaque by Peter Jeffs (Chief Executive YE Yorkshire & Humber); the team had made a small but significant number of sales and everything had been packed away. Right on cue, Fred Gill, a TA from Kelvin Hall, arrived to take us back to Hull. Tired but buoyant we returned home. The KH Smilers first ever road trip had been a massive success.

No sticky white labels for us

Blood, Sweat and Tears

AT school the next day I called a short meeting so that a full report of what had happened at *Venturefest York 2004* could be given to the other three members of the company. As a group we critically examined all that happened during the day, highlighting the positives and examining any negatives. Detailed minutes were kept so that we didn't forget anything that could be of help to us in the future. Looking back, this proved to be a very important meeting, as it spurred us on to work even harder to make KH Smilers the best YE Company in the competition.

The next three months was an incredibly hard and busy period for us all. Not only did we have to keep up with our schoolwork, market and grow several thousand bedding plants but we also had to prepare for the Adjudication Day at the Lawns, in Cottingham, on April 28.

The first thing we did, apart from our GCSE coursework , was to get ourselves invited to as many school functions as possible. In fact, at a previous board meeting we agreed to attend any event at Kelvin Hall School where we could promote the company, sell the old stock and a small range of potted plants, raffle off the odd bay tree and give out as many order forms for our bedding plants as was humanly possible. We even managed to infiltrate a Parents Evening at one of our local feeder primary schools. Targeting these events and meetings proved to be an excellent strategy (brainchild of Mike Jones our Sales Director) as between us we managed to fulfil all four objectives handsomely. Furthermore each director gave out order forms to as many relatives and friends as they could find. Indeed, even though we never managed to sell our total stock of Whacky Test Tubes and Crazy Sand, by the end of April, KH Smilers was debt free (hurray!), had a substantial amount of money in the bank (hurray!) and our order book was full (hurray!). We were not only growing our plants, but also our confidence.

As I have just said the company had sold (but obviously not yet delivered) all of the plants we had grown – some 3000 of them! This was a fantastic achievement. New orders were being received daily throughout February, March and April. The KH Smilers marketing campaign had been an awesome success. The decisions we made way back in January had borne fruit in abundance.

But how were some of these major decisions taken? Well, let me take you back a few weeks and I will try to give you an insight into the decision-making processes within the company. In retrospect, it is clear to see that some of our boardroom decisions virtually made themselves whilst others created lots of healthy argument and debate. To illustrate this point let me give you some examples.

Once we had decided to grow bedding plants (no problems there) the next step was to decide on how many plants to grow and what types. Here the decisions were painless and relatively quick. The number of plants we could grow depended on the shelf space within each greenhouse and the size of containers/carrying trays. Originally we had two greenhouses but then a close friend and near neighbour – Pete Denton - volunteered the use of his greenhouse. That made three. The best containers and associated carrying trays were determined by two factors, advice and price.

Our Finance Director, Richard Myers, was particularly keen to maximise profits by keeping costs low. So, on this basis we eventually chose 7cm pressure formed pots, and carrying trays which were specially designed to support these pots through the growing and marketing stages. Now, some simple maths and hey presto we had the optimum number of plants that could be grown – 3000. Our Operations Director, Benn Jessney, then searched the Internet for the most competitive prices and duly ordered what was needed. Within a week we had the pots/carrying trays in store and ready to use.

Choosing what plants to grow and sell was equally simple. Some research conducted by our Marketing Director, Kathryn Hill, produced a list of the most popular summer bedding plants. Then, as before, we sought horticultural advice before making our decision. The final list included the following plants: Busy Lizzies, Geraniums, Trailing Lobelia, French Marigolds, Pansies, Petunias, Sparaxis, Verbena and Violas. Once again Benn scoured the Internet for the best value plants, eventually settling on a company in Jersey. They supplied all of our plug plants except for the Marigolds which we grew from seed ourselves and the Sparaxis which we grew from bulbs supplied free for placing the order. Richard was particularly happy when we got something for nothing. Making a profit was always the bottom line as far as he was concerned, and freebies that could be sold made good profits!

More problematic were those decisions relating to areas of mixed responsibility. This was because we all had strong opinions on how the company should be run. Similarly, in the matter of aesthetics, we all had opinions on what looked good and what didn't. Sometimes these differences of opinion were difficult to reconcile and as a result, on occasion, people's feelings were hurt and/or their egos bruised. Fortunately, we all knew that KH Smilers was bigger than any one individual and so before long, after the appropriate apologies had been made, we all kissed and made up. Figuratively speaking of course! And then we simply got on with the jobs that had to be done.

By the end of February enough compost for planting just over 3000 plants had been bought and put in to store. However, I won't bore you with the calculations involved in this decision, suffice to say it involved volume and long division. Plants began arriving towards the end of March and continued into early April. Benn checked the plants as soon as they had been delivered and then organised weekend 'planting parties'. Training for this event had already been undertaken at the end of February when we were shown how to plant marigolds from seed. The weather wasn't always kind to us but we had a good laugh whilst we toiled and by mid-April the greenhouses were full of deliciously green and very healthy plants. 'Job done', as Gordon Ramsay would say. All we had to do now was keep them alive until it was time for delivery – mid to late May 2004. A watering rota was established, but as Operations Director, Benn kept a regular check on all the plants so that any diseased or generally unhealthy plants were removed as soon as possible. This was a very important task because as a company we had prohibited the use of pesticides in an attempt to grow our plants as organically as we could. We also undertook various safety measures whilst working in the greenhouses because, as well you know, glass and the human body don't mix that well.

Whilst all this was going on Stu, our ICT Director, grappled with the complexities of producing the KH Smilers web site. We all had input into the content of the site but it was Stu's job to make it a reality. With the aid of a free downloaded template and a bit of advice from Martin Conley at GCS it was soon up and running. Cyber space had its newest addition – www.khsmilers.co.uk. Throughout the competition and beyond Martin freely gave KH

Smilers as much time and practical support as we needed. It was much appreciated.

As if all that wasn't enough we also undertook in-house training during this period with Vic at GCS. Sage UK (a leading supplier of business software worldwide) kindly agreed to let us have a basic accounting package free of charge. Although this was essentially Richard and Mike's territory we all felt that we should understand how the software worked and, more importantly, how it could help our business to be more efficient. Several twilight and weekend sessions later, the company was fully trained and each team member could confidently discuss the software and its contribution to the smooth running of KH Smilers.

Kathryn, Mike, Richard, Dave and Stu with plants

Picture courtesy of Hull Daily Mail

Finally, in early March, Vic arranged for us to do a short presentation about our company to the Wednesday Chapter of Hull's Business Network International (BNI). He explained that obtaining the backing and commercial support of the region's firms would help us make the best possible start. Obviously we agreed immediately. But then came the sting in the tail. The meeting was a 7.00am breakfast meeting and, therefore, we would have to be up and ready to go by 6.30am.

The presentation we devised went down a treat and even though it was very early we clearly impressed this most influential of audiences. As a result when we talked to individual business men and women afterwards, they invariably promised us their backing and as much practical support as we needed. Unfortunately, after such an exciting start to the day, we had to go back to school. After giving up at least two hours of well-deserved sleep we weren't even late for registration. How unlucky was that? However, just a few days later a half page spread in the Hull Daily Mail more than made up for our slice of bad luck (Appendix 1).

Adjudication Day

JUST like *Venturefest York 2004* way back in early February, Wednesday 28 April - Adjudication Day - was on us before we knew it. This was, in fact, a two day process whereby all Hull and East Riding YE teams who had entered into the Company programme were assessed by a panel of judges. Fifteen teams, from eleven different schools, would be put through their paces but only the six winning teams would be allowed to repeat their presentations at the Awards Ceremony at the KC Stadium ('Come on you 'ull') in May. Apart from a couple of extra awards that would be judged at the KC Stadium the rest would be determined that day. We were scheduled to appear at 3.00pm on the final afternoon.

Preparations for this event were intense. To stand any chance of progressing in the competition we had to be one of the chosen six. Everything had to be just right. We were up against schools that had vast experience of this competition whilst we were the new boys (and girl) on the block. Our trade stand had to be informative and eye-catching. Our presentation slick and professional. There could be no room for error. No pressure then!

For the trade stand we felt that simplicity was the key. Something functional but effective. Something aesthetically pleasing but inexpensive. In the days before the competition we experimented with several very different ideas before finally settling on a design which we felt ticked all the boxes. We would try and recreate a scene familiar to anyone who had a back garden. In the centre would be a large garden umbrella. Underneath, a table covered in artificial grass on which we would have order forms, KH Smilers flyers, a laptop running company information, and a large bowl of sweets. To the left and right familiar garden tools – wheel barrow, spade, rake and so on. Posters and photographs would be displayed around the stand and the whole area liberally sprinkled with a range of colourfully planted decorative pots.

Our presentation went through a similar process. Once we decided WHAT we were going to say the only problem would be WHO was going to say it. After much deliberation, and dare I say it, argument, the line up was eventually settled. It would be myself (MD), Kathryn (Marketing), Mike (Sales) and Stu (ICT). Benn would be in charge of the visuals (projected onto a screen behind the presenters) whilst Richard would be our 'super sub', ready to step in at a moment's notice if any one of the presenters could not make it. This really put our negotiating skills to the test!

The visual element of our presentation would be in two sections. First, a PowerPoint presentation which would involve projecting a series of relevant slides on to the screen as each of the presenters spoke. Second, a short video would be embedded towards the end of the presentation showing the team training at GCS with Vic, Benn working in one of the greenhouses, two or three of us potting on plants and then finally, the whole group thanking everyone who had helped so far. Sounded straightforward enough but the timing of our dialogue, so that it would dovetail with the video, was going to be an important consideration. The task was duly completed by Stu with, it must be said, a little advice from Martin.

Rehearsals took place on several occasions, mostly behind closed doors but sometimes in front of a small audience. Under the pressure of trying to get it right tempers often flared and feet were regularly stamped. Constructive criticism wasn't always accepted in the spirit that it was given. However, step by painful step, we could see our performance becoming more and more polished. By the time Adjudication Day arrived we were confident that we had nailed it.

That fateful Wednesday started for us quite early. The team had been given permission to have the day off school (what a bonus!) and we were ready to do battle. The morning was spent rehearsing our presentation and making sure that we had all the elements of our trade stand ready to go. Just after lunch the cars were carefully loaded up and then driven off at speed, snail speed that is. My mum was determined that nothing would get broken whilst she was in charge. Fifteen minutes later, having been overtaken by three cyclists and a man walking his dog, the two cars dribbled to a halt. We had arrived at The Lawns in Cottingham. In truth that must have been the slowest couple of miles ever. I am just thankful that we had taken plenty of sandwiches and something to read.

My mum and Mrs Hill were the first to leave the cars. A quick word was exchanged between the two and then car boots were simultaneously opened. Suddenly the air was pierced by a banshee-like shriek. As one we all turned to look at my mother. Her eyes were fixed on the contents of the boot. Clearly, some disaster had befallen us. We rushed to her side and peered in to the gloom. Eeek! Our star terracotta pot, lovingly made, the centre piece of the trade stand, lay on its side, haemorrhaging plants and compost on to the floor of the boot. For a split second our dreams lay in tatters. Surely, this was a bad omen. KH Smilers had reached the end of the road before it had even got into first gear. But, no. Wait a minute. We were about to be saved. Out of the sky came the unmistakeable figure of 'Potman', protector of planted terracotta pots everywhere. Within seconds the pot was restored to full health and KH Smilers was ready for all and sundry. Thank you Potman, we love you!

If only everything in life was that simple. In reality, of course, we fixed the pot ourselves. Maybe it wasn't quite as good as new but we hoped it would be good enough.

As we entered The Lawns with all our 'stuff' a number of schools had already set up their trade stands. A very impressive sight but I knew ours was better. Well, at least I hoped it was. The team set about building our trade stand quickly. Within a short period of time it was up and running. Colourful and informative, it did everything it said on the tin. A moment was then taken to stand back and admire our handiwork. KH Smilers was ready to meet and greet.

The competition for us that day was against six other teams from four different schools. Pocklington School (Holistic), Cottingham High School (Bags n Boxes & Quick Pix), Sydney Smith School (SYD), and Hymers College (Cushti & Spitting Image). The previous day's competition had involved seven teams from six different schools. Namely, Beverley High School (In Design), Hessle High School (Chicks), Hull High School (Janus & The Full Diamante), Withernsea High School (Starlight), Hull Grammar School (IAI) and South Hunsley School (Aztec).

Hull Grammar School, Hull High School, Hymers College and Pocklington School were all local fee paying schools. The remainder, including Kelvin Hall, were all local senior comprehensive schools, but only ourselves and Sydney Smith were schools within the Hull Local Education Authority.

Time ticked on as we waited for the judges to come to our stand. Eventually they arrived. For a moment it was all smiles and handshakes, but with pleasantries over the questioning began, each question designed to test our knowledge and understanding of how KH Smilers was run and the products that we were selling.

As far as I could tell the whole team fielded individual questions with confidence and clarity. For a few moments as the judges moved on we discussed the experience. We all felt that we had cleared the first hurdle safely. This gave us a huge confidence boost as we prepared to do our presentation.

Dead on 3.00pm the four of us were on the stage just in front of the four or maybe it was five judges. Benn was seated with the projector, entrusted with the task of co-ordinating the PowerPoint presentation with the dialogue from the presenters. Richard, standing behind the judges, offered moral support whilst the unexpected arrival of Mr Doolan offered something familiar to draw strength from. The hour had arrived. It was time to do our thing!

As the projector stirred into action I started speaking. "Good afternoon, and welcome to the KH Smilers company presentation. I am Dave Garbera, Managing Director and you will be meeting the rest of the team shortly. We are all in Y10 at Kelvin Hall School in Hull. The company was founded last September and made a very slow start.......". The familiar words tripped off my tongue easily. As each of us spoke in turn an appropriate slide was seamlessly projected on to the screen behind us. Between the four of us the judges were taken on the rollercoaster ride that was KH Smilers. Accounts and finance, marketing and sales, IT and web site, flyers and posters, Sage training at GCS, planting, Venturefest York 2004, BNI, the Hull Daily Mail, Parents' Evenings, craft fayres, and lots, lots more were all squeezed into the five minute presentation. Before I knew it I found myself repeating the final words of the script. "As you have seen since January the team have enjoyed working together immensely. Hopefully, during this presentation we have given you a flavour of the fortunes of KH Smilers since its creation in September 2003 and will continue to keep on 'Growing a Smile'. On behalf of the whole team I'd like to say thank you, and now I'll let the team have the final word". I turned to face the screen expecting to see the final seconds of a video showing the whole team sat around the garden table toasting all the people who had helped us so far. Instead I saw myself, Richard and Benn potting on some plants. We had been too quick and as a result the video was lagging behind. I turned back to the judges and quipped "In a minute". Everyone laughed and thankfully at that very moment the scene came up. What a relief! There was applause from the judges and an audible sigh of relief from the team. The second hurdle had been cleared.

The third and final hurdle involved a last batch of questions from the judges. Once again answers were given confidently and expertly, apart from one minor hiccup. I had started to answer a question when I suddenly realised I had forgotten what the question was. "Sorry, can you repeat the question?" I asked. In the background I could hear one or two nervous giggles from the team but I stayed focussed, listened carefully and completed the answer magnificently. Well, I thought so anyway. A couple of questions and answers later it was all over and we left the stage. More importantly, however, we were in the home straight heading for the finishing post. But as we crossed the line had we done enough to come in the top six? For that information the team would have to wait until later that evening. First of all the judges would have to get in to a huddle and make their decisions. So the trade stand was duly packed up and we all went back to my house, overtaking cyclists and dog walkers by the dozen. All we could do now was wait and hope that our presentation had convinced them to make KH Smilers one of the six, one of the winners. In the next few hours all would be revealed.

We waited nervously. My eyes kept darting from clock to telephone, from telephone to clock. A cup of tea remained beside me, cold and untouched. Every few minutes someone would get up from their seat and wander aimlessly around the room. I even picked up a copy of 'Kerrang' but found I was reading the same sentence over and over again. As you can imagine no-one felt much like small talk. We just waited. But then, just as day turns into night, the inevitable happened. At 6.00pm the telephone rang. I rushed to pick up the receiver. It was Janet Brumby. I listened intently to her voice. I said goodbye and put the telephone back in its cradle. All eyes were upon me as I sat down. It was good news. No, it was fantastic news! KH Smilers was in the top six and would be presenting at the KC Stadium (Deano! Deano! Deano!) at the Awards Ceremony in May. The team may well have won something but at this stage Janet was not prepared to say any more. The shouts of joy and relief from the team went ringing round the house. Thankfully it was celebration time and not commiseration time. We couldn't have been happier.

As you might imagine my telephone was red hot that evening. I spoke excitedly as I informed every man and his dog that we had been successful. Sleep didn't come easily that night but as I drifted off I realised that KH Smilers had started a journey that could possibly take them to London and the Grand Final at the Savoy Hotel. Dave Garbera, MD, was daring to dream.

KC Stadium

WITH only a week between Adjudication Day and the Awards Ceremony on Thursday 6 May 2004, KH Smilers still had a lot to do. Polish up the presentation, tweek the trade stand, up-date the company report and brush up on any aspects of the business that someone might ask about. Even though we weren't strictly in competition at this event two extra awards were to be presented that night – Best Company Presentation and Best Display on the Evening. Our confidence going in to this event was sky high. We wanted to win everything. But more importantly every member of the team believed that we COULD win everything. It was a fantastic feeling.

The convoy of cars that took us to the KC Stadium arrived just before the event was due to begin. Teams could have access to The Kingston Suite from 4.00pm. Of the 19 schools participating in the Company and Team Programmes that year, fourteen arrived at the KC Stadium. Including KH Smilers, seventeen teams would be assembling their trade stands. Stiff competition for the 'Best Display on the Evening' award, by any stretch of the imagination.

Our display had changed very little since The Lawns in April. As a result it was quickly and efficiently put up. The only small difference was that one of the companies that we had met at Hull BNI back in March – Core Print & Design Services Ltd - had produced a few rolls of yellow sticky 'smiley' badges for us. We stuck a number of these at strategic points on the stand and then gave them out to anyone who would take one. This was only meant to be a bit of fun but it proved to be such an effective marketing and advertising tool on the evening that we continued to use them throughout the remainder of the competition.

Before long the team and our colourful display were ready for action. As one of the six teams performing a Presentation later in the evening, we had also been given the opportunity to have a rehearsal on stage with our PowerPoint slides. Just one change to mention here. Richard stepped in for Mike as one of the presenters. This was not because Mike wasn't available but because we wanted Richard to get some experience of being a presenter just in case he was needed later in the competition. There was now only one thing left to do before the guests (advisers, teachers and parents) arrived to view the trade stands, and that was to eat. The buffet was now open to all achievers. We left the stand and gratefully tucked in.

By 6.00pm we were all back at the stand. For the next thirty to forty minutes we talked to as many people as possible including those who were judging the Best Display of the Evening. At the end of this session it was clear how successful the team had been. Yellow 'smiley' badges could be seen everywhere, even on the lapels of some of the judges!

However, it was time for the evening to move on. Everyone took their seats as Neil Marshall, Chairman of the Hull & East Riding Area Board, gave a brief welcoming address before handing over to Vicki Burton (Area Board Vice Chair) who introduced a review of the Young Enterprise Year. During this review a number of awards were presented but these were outside of the Company Programme. An interval ensued and whilst the audience were treated to music performed by an acoustic duo called Woodsmoke, KH Smilers and the other teams (Chicks, The Full

Diamante, IAI, Bags n Boxes), chosen during the adjudication process, got ready to reprise their Company Presentations. It was show time. We were good that night. Our performance went without a hitch, but whether we were good enough to have produced the best Company Presentation remained to be seen.

The Company Programme Awards started as soon as the Achiever Certificates had been presented to each Company. We, and of course all our supporters, waited with baited breath. First up, Best Display on the Evening. Surely, we had won this. Not even a mention. In the next two categories, Best MD and Best Product or Service, KH Smilers was nominated, but there was no joy to be found here either. Our collective heart sank a little at this point as it dawned upon us that we might not win anything at all. Customer Service Award was fourth. We waited anxiously as the result was announced. "And the winner is.... KH Smilers." Those were the words we had been waiting for. The team jumped for joy as our supporters clapped and cheered. Fifth (Award for Quality) and sixth (Top Achiever) came and went. We were nominated in both but did not win. But before we could feel any sense of loss we won again. This time it was for Financial Accounting. More clapping and cheering as we received the award. The Personnel Award passed us by but the Best Company Report became our third win of the night. Everyone was over the moon. Best Company Presentation was next. Not even a sniff. But before we had any time to dwell on that, KH Smilers was up again. This time the Administration Award was ours. Number twelve, the Marketing Award, slipped through our fingers but thirteen stuck like a limpet. Thirteen maybe unlucky for some but for us it meant that the Multimedia Award was in the bag. We now had five awards safely tucked away. The penultimate award was for the Runners Up in the Hull & East Riding Area competition. All the teams named in this category would get the chance to go to the

Humber final later in the month. Everyone at the KC, teams and supporters, listened intently. One, two, three, four company names were read out. KH Smilers was not amongst them. This could only mean one of two things. We were either going to win the competition of our dreams or our hopes of going to the Humber final were over. I am sure that secretly we all thought it was going to be the latter. After all we were so young! The next moments were heart stopping. As the representative from the HSBC was about to read out the name of the Winning Company we all took a deep breath and held it. The words tumbled out of his mouth but all I heard was the words 'winners', '2004' and 'KH Smilers'. We were ecstatic. Our supporters were beside themselves. KH Smilers had claimed the ultimate prize. We were going to the Humber Final and, possibly more importantly, we were one step closer to the Grand Final at the Savoy Hotel in London.

Before going home the team met briefly with Janet Brumby who supplied us with an information pack that would help us to meet the criteria for the next stage of the competition. For example, one of the instructions required us to get 8 copies of the updated Company Report to Janet within two days. Yup, we thought it was a joke too! This was Thursday night. We were at school the next day and she wanted these reports on Saturday. Maybe getting through to the Humber Final wasn't such a good idea after all!

Soon after 10.00pm the KH Smilers convoy left the KC Stadium physically tired and emotionally drained. That night sleep once again proved difficult to come by, but for Dave Garbera, MD of the WINNING Company, the long term vision remained intact, and the dream was still very much alive.

"Good, aren't they?"

A WEEK later the KH Smilers bandwagon rolled out of town and headed for the Humber Bridge. It was Thursday 13 May. Our destination was Reeds Hotel in Barton; our goal was to win the Humber Strategic Area Final. Within 30 minutes we had rumbled into the hotel car park. My watch revealed it was just turning 3.00pm. According to the timetable we had just 1 hour and 45 minutes to unload the cars, set up the trade stand and rehearse our presentation.

Like a well oiled machine the team went into action. As at every other event the trade stand was assembled quickly but methodically - everything in its place and a place for everything. Once again it oozed colour and efficiency. We had pulled out all the stops to make it a winner. Even the large bowl of sweets looked more seductive than ever.

As time ticked by we were eventually given the opportunity to rehearse our presentation. Mike was back on board for this event and, reassuringly, the practice went without a hitch. After this we went back to the trade stand and waited for our 'fifteen minutes' with the judges. We knew that this part was going to be hard because everyone we had talked to told us it would be. Gulp! But we needn't have worried. Although the questions were tough they were fair, covering every aspect of our business, from finance to sales, from marketing to ICT. No stones were left unturned.

Like fruit passing through a juicer we were squeezed for every last drop of information. By the time we had answered all of their questions we felt somewhat drained but confident that they had gone away suitably impressed. We had shown them that both as a team and as individuals, we knew our business from the inside out.

Invited guests began arriving at about 6.00pm. Our supporters began trickling in soon afterwards, gratefully accepting a glass of wine or orange juice as they entered. I suspect, just like my mum and dad, most of them went for the free wine rather than the juice. But anyway, apart from our parents and 'Grimsta', the KH Smilers guest list included Vic and Martin from GCS and, of course, Mr. Doolan. Taking into account his unexpected appearance at The Lawns, this would be Mr. Doolan's third outing as a KH Smilers groupie. All in all our party was over 20 strong. The prospect of plenty of noise if we won anything at all looked good.

For the next thirty minutes or so everyone milled around, chatting to each other and viewing the trade stands. The atmosphere was beginning to build.

By 6.30pm the audience was seated and Neil Marshall (Strategic Board Chairman) was on stage. He briefly welcomed everyone to the event and wished good luck to all the YE teams. We were under starters orders. A few moments later we were off. The Company Presentations had begun.

First up were Chicks from Hessle High School, then came I.A.I from Hull Grammar School, quickly followed by Myth from John Leggot College (the only school at this event to represent the South Bank of the Humber). They were all good, very good, but there was no time to dwell on that, as it was our turn to present.

As the four of us took our places on the stage I noticed my dad had left his table and found a place in the corner of the room, just to my right. Perched neatly on his shoulder was the most professional looking video camera I had ever seen. He must be moonlighting for the BBC, I thought to myself. I watched him as he squeezed the trigger. At exactly the same time Benn pressed the switch on the projector. It whirred in to life. In seconds the first slide appeared. My brain kicked in to gear and those well practised and familiar words began to flow effortlessly from my mouth. Kathryn, Mike and Stu were equally brilliant as we faultlessly completed our 5 minute presentation. To the sound of applause we left the stage and headed for our seats. "Good, aren't they?" Neil Marshall casually quipped over the microphone. Without sounding too big-headed I must admit that I had to agree with him. However, there was still one team to go, The Full Diamante from Hull High School, and there can be little doubt that their performance was very impressive. Picking up any kind of award at this event was not going to be easy. Winning it was probably impossible!

But for the next hour or so the pressure eased off a little as we were all invited to take a break and have something to eat. As I queued for some food I gazed through the window and across the lake. For the first time that day I realised what a stunningly beautiful location we were in. Even though it was getting rather gloomy I could clearly see the droplets of rain dancing on the surface of the lake. For a brief moment I was totally calm and all was well with the world. But it didn't last long. My thoughts were interrupted by the need to choose a sandwich. I helped myself to more food from the buffet and sat down to eat. Although the team made an effort to chat to everyone, there was only one thing on our minds and that was the Presentation of Awards at 8.15pm. It couldn't come fast enough. We were desperate to know how well or how badly we had done.

At last the appointed hour arrived. Once again my dad was in his corner safely anchored behind his camera. By that time I had learned he had borrowed it from his school. We were all seated at our table willing the results to come our way.

The first award, for the Best Company Display, was presented by Mike Shepherd of Mondi Hypac. We had missed out on this award at the KC Stadium but here in Barton we felt that we had got it absolutely right. As Mike Shepherd finished his address he read out the name of the winner . . . CHICKS. Cheers and applause rang out for this team of girls from Hessle High School. But we had lost this one again. Our supporters sighed and shrugged their shoulders. Was it a sign of worse to come?

Next on stage was Sandra Cooper representing Humber EBLO. She would be making the award for Best Company Presentation. Each team was mentioned in turn and given a positive appraisal. Then she announced the winners. Yes, that's right, I haven't made a mistake. Winners. In the plural. Unable to pick just one team, two were announced . . . The Full Diamante and, wait for it . . . KH Smilers. Thunderous applause and cheering as Stu and a representative from The Full Diamante went to collect the award. However, even though the award was shared it came back to our table. I think that the girls from Hull High School may well have had to break Stu's fingers to prize it from his grasp. Two down and five to go.

Now, full of confidence, we settled down for presentation number three. Wilf Fowler, representing the ICSA, stepped up on to the stage to make the award for Good Governance. After a short speech outlining the importance of good governance he calmly announced the winner . . . KH Smilers. With the sound of people clapping and cheering ringing in his ears Mike went to collect the trophy. He returned to the table with the award and a smile that really did stretch from ear to ear.

The Best Company Report was up next. Enter Andy Tuscher from Business Link Humber. He talked glowingly of the report that had won. A document, he said, that he would have been proud to put before his own Board of Directors. But was this our report? Could it possibly have been that good? Indeed it was. KH Smilers had won again. The noise from our supporters reached another level. I don't think that my feet touched the floor as I went to collect the award. Grinning like a Cheshire cat I returned to my seat.

Onwards and upwards we hit number five, Financial Administration. Presented by Mike Tompkinson of Lloyds TSB, this was one award that our Financial Director, Richard Myers, really, really, really wanted to win. As the short speech drew to an end he talked about the positive impression that everyone had made, but that there was "one company that ticked all the boxes". We waited. He continued. "And that company is KH Smilers". There was an immediate whoop of joy from several of our supporters and then tumultuous applause. Richard sprang to his feet and literally ran to the stage. The Black Horse was finally his. He brought it back to the table as pleased as punch. Four in the bag and two to go.

Pauline Harness was the penultimate person to present an award. Representing The Enterprise Centre (NE Lincs) she was looking to reward the Most Enterprising Company. Once again praise was heaped on all the companies but as is always the case, there could only be one winner (except for the second award, when there were two). The KH Smilers team was confident and geared up for yet another trip to the stage. The swag bag was open and ready to receive the loot. Clear and succinct the name of the winning company shot out of the PA system and reverberated around the room. Funny, it didn't sound like KH Smilers. That's because it wasn't. Instead it was the name of the team from Hull High School.........The Full Diamante. An eruption of clapping and cheering as the announcement was made. Disappointment for us, but the second award of the evening for the girls. However, the drama was not yet over. The final award, the Big One was still to come.

As Tony Lynn from MFI came on to the stage a hush descended over the room. In a few minutes from now the name of the Winning Company would be known. Just as at the KC Stadium these were heart stopping times for all the teams, but being so much younger than the rest of the competition I am sure that we felt it more. He started to speak. I switched off momentarily as I attempted to cross everything that I could. As I returned to the voice coming through the microphone I tuned in to his final words.

"The team that has been selected for this year's Winning Company and that will eventually go forward to the next round at Sheffield, have been selected on their professionalism, the way they have set themselves their own standards, achieved them, and then went on to set themselves higher standards and are looking to achieve them still. The way they applied themselves to all aspects of the criteria that they knew that they would be judged against tonight, and which are fundamentally all the aspects that apply to business practice. And lastly their achievement, and their achievement in adversity, for this particular company had a particularly poor start to their year and have turned their fortunes round phenomenally. So, as we do in the Oscars we'll open the gold envelope....... (there was laughter from the audience, and then a pause as he tore open the envelope and pulled out the contents).........and I would like to invite KH Smilers......" He never finished his sentence. There was uproar. As we snaked up on to the stage to collect the trophy the whole room was applauding, but the support that we had brought with us were clapping and cheering uncontrollably. Most were on their feet, their faces a picture to behold. KH Smilers had done it again. A Year 10 team from a comprehensive school in Hull had swept away all before them. What an achievement! We walked on air for the rest of the evening and talked to anyone who would listen to us.

Before we could 'leave town' the obligatory meeting with Janet Brumby took place. She gave us details of the next round of the competition in Sheffield on Tuesday 15 June. I won't bore you with the details here but, as you can imagine, there was going to be a lot to do. Fortunately, we would have at least a month to do it in.

As usual we had to pack everything away including, after the evening's work, an extra FIVE trophies. Space was tight but we managed it. Shrouded in darkness the KH Smilers convoy

Simply the best!

Picture courtesy of Hull Daily Mail

rumbled out of the car park and headed for home. We crossed the Humber Bridge and left Barton far behind.

That night sleep came more easily to Dave Garbera, MD of the team that had just won the Humber final. He slipped peacefully and effortlessly into his dream. Surrounded by Munchkins and wearing his favourite red slippers, Dave danced his way down the very middle of that Yellow Brick Road, and as he stopped to gaze into the distance the outline of a very posh London hotel appeared to be distinctly closer.

Interregnum

THE next morning, I got up a little earlier than usual. Not because I was so excited that I couldn't sleep any longer, but because Mr Doolan, our esteemed Head teacher, had asked the whole team (plus trophies) to meet him in his office shortly before the formal school day actually started. We had done this before. Exactly one week earlier to be precise (after the KC Stadium). The time had come, for what I later dubbed, the Grand Parade. It was Mr Doolan's opportunity to show us, and our achievements, off to the whole staff. Slightly apprehensive, but well prepared by our previous experience, KH Smilers entered the belly of the beast. Yes, we were in the staffroom again, surrounded by hordes of teachers. Silence descended. Mr Doolan, chest puffed out, and as pleased as any one of us, recounted the events of the night before. Once again we basked in their admiration. To the sound of applause still ringing in our ears we left the inner sanctum, separated and went to our different tutor groups. We were back in the world of teachers, books, lessons and homework. Oh, joy!

Within a day or two, the news of our success in Barton had spread around Hull. We were receiving messages of congratulations every day. Many were from members of the local business community whom we had met through Hull BNI, whilst others came from Hull City councillors like Sheila Waudby. Even the Lord Mayor of Kingston upon Hull and Admiral of the Humber (to give him his full title), Councillor Ken Branson, was prepared to recognise our achievement – twice! First, by offering to let us be the first young people to attend and participate in a full meeting of the Hull City Council, and second by inviting us back later in the month to attend a buffet reception in the Dining Room of the Guildhall. Each member of the team even received a commemorative Kingston upon Hull letter opener and pencil set after the first visit. I've still got mine. It's in mint condition and destined to be a family heirloom. Oh yes, and another half page spread in the Hull Daily Mail (Appendix 2).

As it was now the middle of May our plants were looking better than ever. There had been few casualties and preparations were made for deliveries to take place. Customers were always telephoned beforehand and convenient times arranged. Any address within walking distance we took care of ourselves, even though on some occasions it meant three or four of us turning up on someone's doorstep. Now and again we used a wheelbarrow. Embarrassing, I know, but it had to be done. Deliveries further afield had to be co-ordinated with available transport. None of us were old enough to drive so we had to rely on our parents and Vic to help us out. They never let us down. However, at least one member of the team would always be there to make the actual delivery and collect the money. All of our transactions were cash on delivery. This was a decision we took back in January. We felt that this would give our customers some peace of mind. They could order plants knowing that if we didn't deliver it wouldn't cost them a penny. In essence, it was a totally risk free operation for the customer. This strategy worked very well and we never had any problems. Moreover, it gave Richard something to count at the end of each day. By the time we left for Sheffield on 15 June our greenhouses were virtually empty. Weeks of worrying finally ceased. Three thousand plants were now happy in their new homes.

Preparations for the regional final in Sheffield carried on throughout the delivery period. As ever the Company Report had to be updated, but this time, instead of going to Janet, nine copies had to be sent to the YE offices in Leeds by Wednesday 2 June. Unfortunately, due to a mixture of procrastination and dithering on our part the report wasn't finished until the night of Tuesday 1. Sending the copies by post was now out of the question. There was only one thing for it. Someone had to take it. But who would have the time or the inclination to do that? A list was drawn up. Name after name was crossed out until only one remained, Di Garbera, my mother. At this point the rest of the team went home and I switched to begging mode.

Actually she didn't need much persuasion at all. Staying in the competition was just as important to her as it was for us. However, getting to the YE offices in Yeadon was a different story altogether. Bad weather, missed turnings and poor directions combined to make it a very fraught and tense journey. In the end she made it by the skin of her teeth. The offices were just minutes away from closing when she arrived with our precious cargo. It was close, very close but we were still in the competition.

During this time KH Smilers also produced two newsletters (in May and June) for our customers and shareholders. Called 'Cuttings from the Greenhouse', it was printed on glossy paper and in colour. With a mixture of pictures, news and current information about KH Smilers we hoped to give our supporters a flavour of the experiences we were having; giving them an opportunity to feel part of the company that they had helped to make so successful. And judging by the feedback we received the newsletters went down wonderfully well.

Soon after our win at Barton, the team paid a return visit to the Wednesday Chapter of Hull BNI. Once again we were made very welcome and our haul of trophies was much admired by all the members. Casual conversations with the business men and women who were there that morning, resulted in many words of encouragement and offers of practical support. We received both with eagerness and much gratitude.

On Saturday 29 May, the 'Smilers' organised a social event at the local pub, the Goodfellowship. It had a two-fold purpose. First, was to thank our shareholders, family and friends for all the help and support they had given us; and second was to raise as much money as possible for the Candlelighters, a charity that supports children with leukaemia. It exceeded all of our expectations. The proceeds from the tombola, auction, quiz and raffle totalled more than £700. And equally as important everyone who attended had a great time.

Another welcome distraction from the pressures of competition was our day at the spectacular Yorkshire International Business Conference, held at the KC Stadium (Appendix 3). We had been invited to attend on Friday 11 June. Although we were split up on arrival we didn't mind as we found ourselves sitting with some of the region's most influential people. In fact we spent the whole day mingling with business entrepreneurs like Yorkshire's Paul Sewell, and international figures such as Hans Blix, William Hague and Chief Solutions Officer of Yahoo!, Tim Sanders. An immensely enjoyable day was had by all. As we left I secretly hoped that we would be back next year. We were now used to events like this and so I didn't find them quite as daunting anymore!

Throughout, we continued to work on our presentation. Although we tweaked the script and PowerPoint here and there, essentially it stayed the same. It was simply a matter of updating certain aspects of the company profile, for example, finance and sales. On the other hand our performance continued to develop and change. The more we rehearsed the more confident and professional our delivery became. This process, however, was not without its dangers and produced its fair share of short tempers, tantrums and heated exchanges. But invariably we got over it and moved on. No matter how much we bickered and/or sulked during our 'creative phases' we were always friends afterwards. That was very important to us all.

The trade stand was our biggest change. After failing to win awards for our stand on two occasions we felt that this was a weakness we had to address. Moreover, although there would be no specific award for the best trade stand at Sheffield, it would be one of the three main criteria (Company Report and Presentation

Three Smilers meet Paul Sewell

Picture courtesy of Hull Daily Mail

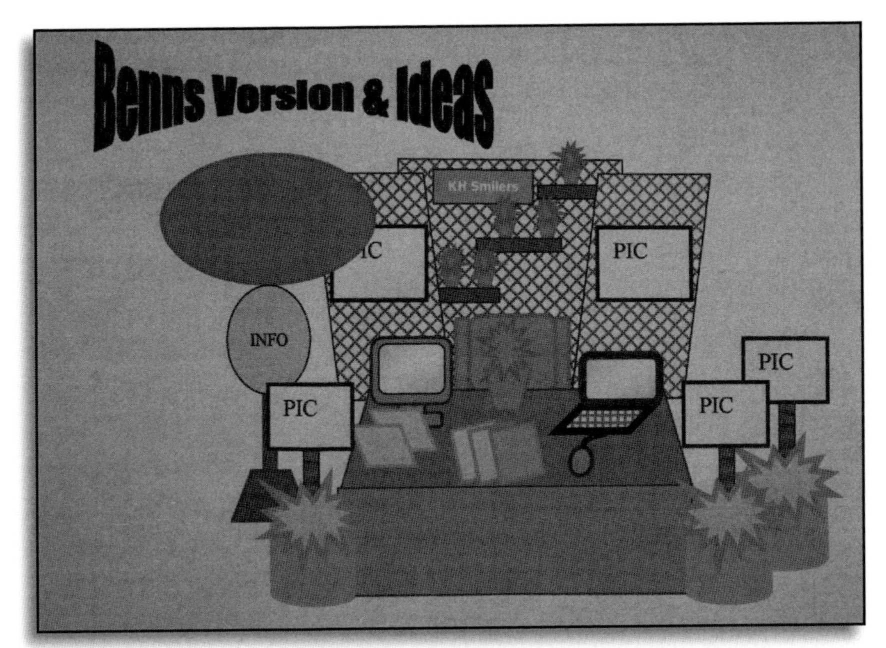

Benn's design for the new trade stand

being the other two) that we would be judged against in the battle for the Best Company in the Yorkshire and Humber region. Or to put it another way, the best YE company within an area of 5953 square miles and 5.2 million people. Nerdy, I know, but absolutely true.

To get us on the right track the team had a free consultation with Mary Wells of MW Design & Marketing Ltd, a Hull BNI member whom we had met earlier in the year. This meeting gave us plenty of food for thought. However, Benn must have been particularly inspired because he came back the next day with his vision of what the stand should look like. Computer-generated and fully labelled, it was brilliant. It became the blueprint for the next KH Smilers trade stand. We set about trying to recreate it immediately. Sheffield was now less than two weeks away.

The City of Steel

TICK. Tock. Tick. Tock. Tick. Tock. The relentless sound of time flowing imperceptibly into the future. Tuesday June 15 2004 dawned to the sound of twittering birds, my mum having her daily shower and a strange mix of Viking FM and Radio Humberside. My dad liked Andy Comfort on Humberside, I preferred the music of Viking, but as far as my mother was concerned, I can only suppose that she just liked to keep clean. As my eyes adjusted to the morning light filtering through into my room, my dad stuck his head around the door, wished me luck for Sheffield, and disappeared off to work. I, in turn plumped up my pillow, pulled my cover tight and snuggled down for a few more minutes of well-deserved sleep. But to no avail. My mother's twin-engined, turbo charged, fuel injected hair dryer screamed and screeched into action. It was definitely time to get up!

By mid-morning the whole team had assembled – three cars, three drivers and six 'Smilers'. With great excitement we checked the new trade stand. It was all there and ready to be loaded in to the waiting cars. In less time than it takes to learn Ancient Greek it was done. Everything else, including our 'uniforms', followed in quick succession. Each item had been ticked off. Nothing had been left to chance. Once again the KH Smilers juggernaut was ready to roll. Mirror. Signal. Manoeuvre. As each driver entered the flow of traffic the ritual was performed perfectly. The City of Steel was calling.

Moments later we were trundling down the M62. Each of us, locked in our own thoughts, as well as in different cars, staring out of the windows as the countryside whipped by. Eventually we slipped on to the M18, then the M1 before finally cruising into the city on the Sheffield Parkway. We had made good time and all was going well. That is, until we hit Park Square and entered the nightmare world of...........the one way system. In minutes we were hopelessly lost and engaged in a war of attrition with heavy afternoon traffic. It took several phone calls (between cars), numerous hand gestures and the odd expletive before we finally pulled up in front of the Cutlers' Hall. And to top it all, nowhere to park and double yellow lines everywhere.

Like a squad of Olympic athletes we jumped out on to the pavement and began unloading the cars in double quick time. Before any jobsworth could say those immortal words "I'm afraid you can't park here, Sir!" the drivers and their cars had gone, and KH Smilers was ready for business.

We entered the building. With sherpas in tow and oxygen masks at the ready, we were ushered up the Everest of all staircases, in to the Drawing Room (very posh, like being in the room of a stately home) and shown where to position our trade stand. The space was exactly 2 metres square and contained a single uncovered table. According to the itinerary, the team would have a couple of hours, including some rehearsal time, to set up the stand. Judging would begin at 3.00pm. There was no time to lose. Assembling the new trade stand had to be our first priority.

The first thing we did was to move the table to the front of our square, and cover it with artificial grass. Then a huge green garden umbrella was put up behind the table. This was enclosed by three large trellis panels carefully hinged together. The whole framework was then locked together by using a fourth arched panel screwed across the top. This carried the company name, KH Smilers. Each letter of the name had been made from bright yellow artificial flowers and carefully pinned in to place. Finally, the whole area was dressed with photographs, previous awards, posters, newsletters, laptop, hanging baskets, pots and lots and lots of flowers. Subtle lighting completed the picture. The finished product was magnificent. A winner if ever I saw one!

At the same time, of course, the three other Area winners were putting the finishing touches to their trade stands. Representing North Yorkshire was Skipton Girls' High School (IDentity); winners of the South Yorkshire competition was Doncaster College (CCPS) and Leeds Grammar School (Gold Chip Enterprises) had come from West Yorkshire. This was formidable opposition.

Before the judges came to inspect the stand and interview the team (sometime between 3.00pm and 4.00pm) KH Smilers had their opportunity to rehearse the presentation. As usual all went well, and we went back to the trade stand quietly confident that we could produce a winning performance later in the evening.

In groups of three the judges began their tour of inspection and inquisition. For the next hour or so we would be under the microscope. The trade stand looked gorgeous. Warm and colourful, friendly and inviting, it had success written all over it. We didn't look too bad either. I was sure that the whole package would impress the judges. I was equally sure that as a team, and as individuals, we would interview well. Our communication skills had improved greatly over the last few months, and we were far more relaxed.

Once our inquisitors had returned to their lair we compared notes. It soon emerged that we had answered some difficult and probing questions about the company, and the whole YE experience with confidence and passion. However, we were all relieved when this part, probably the most testing and difficult part of the competition, was over. But, only time would tell, if our pain and suffering had been worth it.

Right on time the guests started to arrive. It was now about 4.30pm. The KH Smilers party, including ourselves, would be fifteen strong. Not many I agree, but due to the nature of the event that was all that we were allowed. At this point everyone was given the chance to have a chat and view the stands. Company Presentations would take place one hour later at 5.30pm.

Once the audience had been seated and welcomes made, the presentations began. Gold Chip Enterprises from Leeds Grammar School presented first. They were followed by IDentity from Skipton Girls' High School. We featured third and CCPS (Car Crime Protection Squad) from Doncaster College completed the line up. Each team's performance, including our own, was assured and professional. This was going to be a very difficult one to call.

The formal dinner took place in the Old Banqueting Hall at 7.30pm. Beautifully laid out in a splendid room this meal would severely challenge my knowledge of what to use and when. Each table was awash with cutlery and glasses. It was more daunting than any of the competitions I had been in so far. I resigned myself to observing my fellow diners for those essential etiquette rules. Not that any of the 'Smilers' would have a clue, but Mr Doolan, one of our invited guests and sitting at our table, would make the perfect mentor. My worries were over.

The menu looked delicious. But don't worry, for this section I've put on an extra large, absorbent bib and I promise not to howl. For the starter we had a choice of two dishes served with a selection of freshly baked breads. Terrine of salmon and asparagus with a compote of tomatoes and rocket pesto OR individual mini pasties of meat and potato, smoked haddock, prawn and leek. The main meal was described as 'The Best' Yorkshire pork and herb sausages, mashed potato with wholegrain mustard and red onion gravy served with a selection of vegetables: roasted carrots, sugar snap peas and saute courgettes. Finally, a choice of four desserts: mini lemon tart, chocolate casket with red cherries in Kirsch, shot glass of strawberry & sparkling wine OR passion fruit cheescake. What a feast! In fact the diners enjoyed the meal so much that the chefs were invited to receive the customary sign of appreciation. As they filed out from the kitchen and assembled at the front of the stage they were given a huge round of applause. In my opinion, it was thoroughly deserved.

The meal completed and cleared away it was time for the speeches and awards. There were to be six awards given that evening but only three which directly involved the four teams in the YE Company Programme.

The first was an individual award and would be presented to the MD with the best all round skills. Based on the Company Report and interviews with the Company members, particularly the MD, it also carried with it a cheque for £100. I was very nervous at this stage. This would be my first individual award. I listened intently to the speaker but not really hearing what he was saying. There was a pause. A name was read out. It took a few moments to register. Everybody around me was clapping and cheering. Yes, he definitely said it, he definitely said my name, David Garbera. I was speechless. All smiles and pride I got up to collect my award. The trophy of a small inscribed glass pyramid was brilliant, but the envelope with a cheque inside felt equally good.

The second of the Company Programme awards was for Good Governance. KH Smilers had won this award in Barton and so we were reasonably confident that we could do it again. Nerves jangling we sat through the short speech. Again there was a slight pause as the winning name was read out. Alas, it was not the name we were hoping for. Instead, it was Skipton Girls' High School that were celebrating their first win. If we were disappointed we didn't show it. The most important award, The Nestle Shield (and cheque for £200) for the Best Company, was still to come. Game on.

By this time the team and all our supporters were a bag of nerves. The atmosphere in The Banqueting Hall was electric as the final speaker began his address. One hundred people were perched on the edges of their seats as they waited for the most terrifying announcement of the night. As the envelope appeared the tension in the room was at fever pitch. Suddenly, for me, everything went into slow motion. The sound of tearing as the envelope was opened. The muffled crumpling noise as he pulled out the contents. The opening and closing of his mouth as he began to speak. Kaaaaaaa Aiiiiiiitch Smiiiiiiileeeeeeers. Uproar. Real time kicked back into gear. We got to our feet. Our supporters got to their feet. As everyone in the room continued to clap and cheer the six grinning 'Smilers' headed for the podium. What a moment. We were now officially the best YE Company in Yorkshire and Humber.

The actual presentation was made by John Healey, Economic Secretary to the Treasury. Nice man. We were also presented to the Lord Mayor of Sheffield. Nice woman. A representative from the HSBC also rewarded us with a huge luggage label. The address on it read: The Savoy, Strand, London. KH Smilers had done it. We had reached the Grand Final.

Trillions of photographs later we had our usual meeting with Janet Brumby. It followed a familiar pattern. Many congratulations from her and a pack of information for us. By now, however, it was getting late. The event had overrun by at least one hour and

London here we come

we still had the trade stand to take down and pack away. Exhausted we left Sheffield about midnight. Ninety minutes later I was happily tucked in bed.

Quicker than you can say 'Dad, can you take us to see Rammstein in Copenhagen', Dave Garbera, MD of the best YE Company in Yorkshire and Humber, was fast asleep. As the door to his dream world opened wide the Munchkins were already in party mood. He raced to join them but in his haste he failed to notice an unconscious Ewok (don't ask) in the middle of the Yellow Brick Road. He tripped and fell. Tumbling over and over, the wall of a large building suddenly brought him to an abrupt halt. Looking up at the facade he saw five huge golden letters:

SAVOY

Smugly he turned over in his bed. On Tuesday 13 July 2004 his audacious dream to be in the YE Grand Final in the Savoy Hotel would finally become a reality.

Interregnum II

HERE we go again. It was time for Grand Parade Number 3. Usual routine. Basking. Separation. Double Maths. Oh, and while I remember, yet another half page article in the Hull Daily Mail (Appendix 4).

In the month before travelling to London, KH Smilers had a lot to do. Fortunately, we were spared the effort of having to update the Company Report. The rules of the competition clearly stated that no amendments could be made after the Regional Final. Indeed, a copy of the report had to be given to a representative from Young Enterprise UK National Office on the day of our competition in Sheffield. At least we couldn't be late with this one!

Our trade stand was second to none at Sheffield but it took us rather too long to assemble on the day. Therefore, over the next four weeks the team spent many hours erecting and dismantling the stand. The practise, however, paid off. By the time we shipped it off to London for the Grand Final, we could put it together not only in record time but, if needs be, with our eyes tight shut. Although the content of the stand changed a little, we felt that no major changes were necessary.

We took a similar view of our presentation. Minor changes were necessary but that was all. Our performance, on the other hand, could always be improved. On that basis we put in many more hours of rehearsal time, and on one occasion my dad even videoed these performances so we could see for ourselves what the audience would be watching. It proved to be a most useful training tool.

Up until now we had stuck with our original uniform – white shirt, blue tie, black trousers and shoes. However, after some discussion at one of our Board meetings the team felt we still looked too much like school kids and not enough like members of the business community. Within minutes it was agreed. We would all dress in suits. KH Smilers would become the Men (and one woman) in Black. Smart and professional to the core.

Events. There were a few. But not too few to mention. We did what we had to do, and attended each one without exception. Remind you of a song? Yes, well, altogether now. But more, much more than this, we did it our way.

The first event was on the evening after the Regional final. We returned to school at 7.00pm that Wednesday ready to do our presentation for the Governing Body. Armed with all our awards, the team reproduced our winning Company Presentation for the assembled members. Applause greeted the end of the performance. They were then very liberal with their praise and wished us well for the Grand Final. Suitably impressed by the experience we picked up our trophies and left. Goodness knows what it would have been like if the 'Smilers' had lost in Sheffield.

For the second event we returned to the scene of our first triumph. The KC Stadium. This was not a YE function but one staged by Humber EBLO, an organisation that links education and business. The awards were being held to recognise and reward significant contributions made by young people, teachers, employees and businesses involved in Education Business Link activities over the previous academic year. This was a most prestigious occasion. KH Smilers was invited to attend the function for two reasons.

Picture courtesy of Hull Daily Mail **Contents of the swag bag revealed**

Firstly, we had been commissioned to provide twenty five table decorations for the 250 specially invited guests. These had a blue and silver theme and were displayed on all of the tables throughout the evening. Not only were we paid by the event organisers for supplying the potted plants, but then at the end of the night we sold the lot to the guests! So in fact we managed to sell the same thing twice. Now that's what I call business acumen, and what a profit! Actually we did have permission, but it was our idea.

Secondly, to support yours truly, who had been nominated to receive the Award for Enterprise – Young Person. This award was to be given to the young person who had shown significant flair and determination in the Young Enterprise Programme. That would be me then!

Dressed in our 'Company Presentation uniforms', we arrived shortly before the 6.00pm start so that we would have enough time to put out all the table decorations. It was Thursday 8 July. The Master of Ceremonies for the evening was the one and only, the legendary Andy Comfort, Radio Humberside DJ and supporter of the Tractor Boys. Only slightly less well known was the main speaker, Gill Adams, playwright and journalist for the Hull Daily Mail.

Once more I can't resist telling you about the menu for the evening. (Grrrrr). Cream of wild mushroom & herb soup, breast of chicken with caramelised baby onion & tarragon sauce and last but not least, chantilly cream-filled profiteroles with a rich Belgian chocolate sauce. Delightful.

The awards themselves were given in several different categories. The Award for Enterprise was the second category to be presented. With a very eloquent introduction from Andy Comfort I went up to receive my framed certificate. Although this was not a competition as such - I knew that I had won before the event - I still had a few butterflies before the announcement was made. Moreover, hearing the applause and maintaining a winning streak was very good for my moral.

Throughout the evening I kept an eye on my dad. I knew that at some point in the evening he would not be able to resist seeking out his local DJ hero, Andy Comfort. And I was right. At the end of the evening when Andy was mingling with the guests he made a beeline for him. I was a few paces behind. He introduced himself and exchanged pleasantries. So far, so good. But then he uttered that most inane of statements. "If I may say so, you don't look like you sound". How embarrassing! I disappeared before I heard Andy Comfort's response, but as I sped away I muttered to myself, "I bet he's never heard that one before". It was definitely time to go home.

KH Smilers had one more decision to make before leaving for London. It was always going to be a difficult one to make so we put off making it for week after week after week. Eventually, however, there was no escape and the situation had to be resolved. Let me explain.

The rules for the YE Company Programme stated that a team wishing to enter the competition had to have a minimum of six members. No problem there. KH Smilers had been able to comply with that rule from September 2003 when there was a team of eighteen. Unfortunately, for one reason or another, that was down to the bare minimum by January 2004. Still no problem. The team was perfectly legal. It was only when the rules for the Grand Final were examined in more detail that alarm bells began to ring. One of the rules clearly stated that any team winning through to the London final could only send a team of FIVE. We immediately consulted with Janet Brumby who confirmed our worst nightmare. One of the 'Smilers' would indeed have to be dropped from the squad and would not be able to travel to the Savoy. We were stunned. How could we possibly take that kind of decision and rob one of our own of this fantastic opportunity? Someone who had shared in all the hard work and dreamt of the ultimate prize would have to stay at home. No way. It was grossly unfair and as a team we resolved it was not going to happen. Even though one of us would not be able to compete we would all be going to London. Somehow, no matter what the cost to the company, the six 'Smilers' who had started the journey in January would be the same six 'Smilers' that would finish it in July!

91 The Strand

SUNDAY 11 July 2004 was going to be a busy day. For my parents and me the morning started very early. Courtesy of Young Enterprise, who would be footing the bill, KH Smilers was able to hire a driver and van to take our trade stand to London. He arrived on our doorstep at about 7.00am. With the van doors wide open, the driver waited to receive his precious cargo. Meanwhile my dad and I had gone round to the back of the house to fetch one of the large trellis panels. As we came round the corner and approached the van my dad stopped dead in his tracks. The driver looked at my dad, my dad looked at the van. He was convinced that the van was too small. The driver took a little bit more convincing. However, he eventually agreed that even though we could get the first panel into the van, there was no way another three panels and then all the other paraphernalia would fit. He left promising to return with a bigger van, IF there was one in the yard. Yikes! All we could do was wait and hope.

As good as his word he did return and with a bigger van. He had saved the day. In anticipation of his successful return we had brought the complete trade stand and more to the front of the house. Within an hour we had loaded the van with a mountain of stuff and waved him off. Hopefully, we would be reunited with the driver, and the contents of his van later in the day.

At 10.11am precisely the train pulled out of Paragon Station. On board were ALL the 'Smilers', my mum (chaperon and general dogs body), the 'Grimsta' (she had decided to have a break in London that weekend as it was going to be her birthday on the 13th) and Benn's mum and dad, Julie and Tony (supporters). Richard amused himself by keeping a video diary whilst the rest of us busied ourselves by doing absolutely nothing. The most strenuous thing any of us probably did was to turn our heads to watch the English countryside go racing by. Clickity, clack. Clickity, clack. Clickity, clack. The train sped towards London. At 13.03pm exactly we pulled into King's Cross Station. Preparations for the final phase of the competition could now begin.

A tube ride later we were outside The Strand Palace Hotel, our base for the next four days. The Savoy was just across the road. Laden down with bags we snaked into the hotel and booked in. Excitedly we disappeared to our rooms to unpack. I shared a room with Stu whilst Mike shared with Benn. Richard and Kathryn had their own rooms. It wasn't the largest or most luxurious hotel room I had ever stayed in, but as we were only going to use it for sleeping in and somewhere to get changed I don't suppose it really mattered. It was compact but functional.

At 2.45pm we left the hotel and crossed The Strand towards the Savoy. It was a warm and bright Sunday afternoon. The driver of the van was supposed to meet us outside the River Entrance by 3.00pm so we didn't want to be late. No van as we arrived. We waited. As vehicles turned the corner and came down the street we all turned expectantly, hoping to see the van and a familiar face behind the wheel. No luck. We continued to wait. Nervous glances were being exchanged. Watches were constantly monitored. Feet shuffled as the team became more and more agitated. Although nothing was said out loud I knew that we were all thinking the same thing. We were all contemplating the dire consequences of his non-arrival. Deep in thought, quiet descended on the group. Suddenly someone's mobile shrieked into life. There was a sharp intake of breath. We were all eyes and ears as my mum answered the call. It was the driver. Our hearts soared. He was lost. Our hearts sank. He was at the front of the Savoy (yippee!) but didn't know how to get round the back (ohhh!). For a split second it was all doom and gloom again. But then I realised that we had just made that exact same journey from the Strand Palace. Quickly my mum gave him the directions. Everyone breathed a huge sigh of relief. There were smiles all round as the mobile disappeared into the cavern that was my mother's hand bag. The panic was over.

Moments later as the van turned the corner there was a huge spontaneous cheer from the group. We were so pleased to see him that unloading the van was more of a pleasure than a chore. Everything intact, we deposited the unassembled trade stand inside the hotel and then said our goodbyes to my mum, the 'Grimsta' and Richard. Unfortunately, our Financial Director would not be helping us to build the stand. Although he had come with us to London we had reluctantly decided that he would not be part of the five-strong presentation team, and as a result he was excluded from this part of the competition.

As we entered the Lincoln Room to put up our trade stand it was a hive of activity. Dozens of excited young people from eleven other companies were already busy constructing their displays. It was at this point that the reality of the situation hit us like a bolt from the blue. I can distinctly remember feeling very young and, possibly, out of my depth. Everyone else looked so much older. Fortunately, we didn't have time to dwell on this and quickly found our allotted space and set to work. Progress was deliberately slow. We were determined to build a trade stand that would rival and successfully compete with the other eleven in the room. I took a few moments to survey the scene. As the youngest

At the Savoy - setting up the stand

team at the Savoy I knew it wasn't going to be easy. After all, including KH Smilers, these were the best twelve teams in the United Kingdom. Three thousand five hundred had been whittled down to a dozen. Even if we didn't win anything at all it was a privilege to be here.

We knew something about each team because, as regional winners, we had all been featured in a column in The Times, but this was the first time we had come face-to-face with our rivals for the big prize. I scanned each of our opponents in turn.

S.O.S. – Beanie hats, wallets and a computer game called "School Quest Delta" - were from the Christian Brothers Grammar School in Northern Ireland.

Representing London were St Paul's School with a company called OCCASIO – "Rag Bags" made from second-hand suit jackets and an image library.

Ysgol Tre-Gib from Wales gave us UNDERWOOD VISIONS – a Dylan Thomas virtual tour on CD Rom.

From the West Midlands, John Taylor High School brought RAIR – a shot glass freezer mould and "Party in a Box".

PATHWAYS – lenticular lamp, L.E.D. cups, illusions game – came from Westhoughton High School in the North West.

South West regional winners were ZEPHYR – granite coasters and paperweights, B-Boards, "Wobblies" and novelty pencils - from Truro School.

All the way from Scotland came Stromness Academy with their company ORKNEY INK – tourist guide book "A Week in Orkney".

Representing the East of England were LEAF IT – hand-decorated terracotta pots with plants, Christmas cards – from Northgate High School.

GENESIS – "The Teen Guide" photography, beanies (hats) and a Valentine Disco – were from the Royal Grammar School, Guildford in the South East.

Ockbrook School from the East Midlands came with a company called PINK ZEBRA – candles, photo frames and jewellery.

Last but not least BLINK – blue and pink themed pens & pencils, photo frames, greetings cards and soap – from Westfield School in the North East.

And I thought Sheffield was tough! However, my few moments of idleness came to a swift end as all the teams were called into the Parlour for afternoon tea and a briefing. Chattering excitedly we all went into the room. Everyone helped themselves to a drink and biscuits. Once the sixty or so students were settled Peter Westgarth (Chief Executive, Young Enterprise) welcomed us all to the Savoy and congratulated the teams on winning through to the Grand Final. Moreover, he made it quite clear that even if individual companies were not successful during this competition, the fact that we were here at all was a fantastic achievement. He was right of course, but at that moment in time I don't believe there was a single person in the room who thought that in two days time they might be going home with nothing. He then went on to describe the different aspects and processes of the competition before finally wishing us all good luck. As Peter Westgarth left, the teams went back to complete their trade stands. By 6.00pm the five of us had finished. There was no more we could do. The stand looked magnificent. The best one yet. We kissed it good-night and left for the Strand Palace. This would be followed by an evening in London.

Back at the hotel we all went to our separate rooms. Washed and changed the whole party met up in the lobby. Mr Doolan, official chaperon and link teacher, had arrived whilst we were at the Savoy. He would also be out with us for the evening. The eleven of us headed for the Covent Garden tube station and our first port of call, The London Eye.

After just a few stops and a change of line, we finally emerged into the early evening sunshine from the station at Waterloo. This had taken us straight to the Eye. Tickets were booked as soon as we arrived and at 8.00pm the six 'Smilers' were on board. Views to the north, south, east and west were breathtaking. The whole of London seemed to be laid out before us. We just didn't know where to look next as the panorama unfolded before our very eyes. Unable to contain our enthusiasm we found ourselves pointing, shouting and taking photographs all at the same time. It was a marvellous experience. Unfortunately, after just thirty minutes the flight was over. Back on terra firma our stomachs were telling us that it was time to eat. We also noticed that our group had swelled to twelve. Vic Golding, our business adviser, had joined us. He had been in London since Friday on a family visit, so we simply arranged to meet up with him at the London Eye on the Sunday evening.

As we made our way towards Piccadilly for something to eat a problem began to emerge. Where should we actually eat? At this point my mother suggested Adam's Rib, a place that we had been to before and always found good value for money. It was agreed. We would go there first. However, before we had even set foot in the place, some of the party thought that it would be a good idea to have a quick look around, just to see what else might be available. The quick look turned into an hour's aimless walkabout, and with still no consensus in sight it was decided that we should go back to where we had begun, Adam's Rib. It was 10.00pm by this time and everybody was starving. Orders were placed with uncommon haste and within a short period of time most of us were tucking into something hot and delicious. Three courses were soon devoured and we left to catch the next available tube train to Covent Garden. Just after midnight we were walking down The Strand towards our hotel. Moments later we were all in bed fast asleep.

That night there was no dream for Dave Garbera, MD of KH Smilers, finalists at the Savoy, it was more of a sound sensation. As he drifted off to sleep his head was filled with the voice of Brian Ferry and his band Roxy Music, singing their classic 1970's hit 'Do the Strand'. Moments later the clock radio switched into silent mode, and silence filled the room.

The Final Countdown

MONDAY 12 July was another fine day. Everybody was up bright and early for breakfast. By 8.30am we were suited up and making our way towards the Savoy. We were ready to compete.

When we got to the trade stand everything looked fine. Down the centre of the room the judges' tables had already been neatly laid out. We would be allowed a further 45 minutes to make any final preparations. Stu set up the laptop whilst the rest of us checked the plants. Any blemished flowers or leaves were nipped out and disposed of. Our trademark bowl of sweets was filled to overflowing, and with a final splash of water for the blooms everything was ready for the judges. There was no more to be done.

At 9.30am all the teams made their way to the Manhattan Room. This included Mr Doolan and Vic. As link teacher and business adviser respectively they would be allowed to stay with us all day. Everybody would be in there for the next two hours. During this time each company would have the opportunity to rehearse their presentation in the Ballroom. KH Smilers turn came just after 10.00am. Everything went to plan. Not a hitch in sight. Well, maybe there was one minor hiccup. As Stu stepped back from the podium to leave the stage he had a slight altercation with an up-lighter. He sent it crashing to the floor. Fortunately, neither Stu nor the up-lighter received any long term injury. The up-lighter was returned to its former upright position but no longer sending out any light, and Stu left the stage. Otherwise our whole performance was flawless and exuded bags of confidence. We were very pleased. The team returned to the Manhattan Room as Morning Coffee was being served. Just what we needed after our little bit of excitement in the Ballroom. Stu in particular deserved his drink. After all, it's not every day that you knockout an up-lighter with a single blow. He literally punched its lights out. What a man!

Free time was over by 11.30am. All twelve teams were instructed to return to their respective trade stands and prepare themselves for the judging session. The real test was now about to begin. For the next one and a half hours KH Smilers would be bombarded with questions designed to find how well we actually knew our business, and what skills we had developed as a result of being involved in the YE Company Programme.

Back at the stand Vic casually suggested we set up the laptop fairly quickly, as one of the judges could arrive at any moment. We had all seen Stu set it up earlier that morning, so we knew that there was nothing to worry about, but as we turned to confirm its presence, Vic was right, it was not there. Everybody did a quick, but thorough search. Nothing. There was only one explanation. It had been stolen. But before we pressed all the alarm bells we noticed many of the teams were in a similar flustered condition. It transpired that other laptops had also gone. The potential for panic was immense. Fortunately, within minutes the mystery had been solved and the computers returned. Whilst everyone was in the Manhattan Room an over-zealous YE official had decided that all the unattended laptops might not be safe, so he promptly disconnected each one and put the lot in a secure store. Happily, this proved to be no more than a minor inconvenience. With nerves suitably settled the competition could proceed.

Each of the five judges – John Rendall (Chair), Adrian Tripp,

Lee Williams, Stephen Lyle Smythe and Caroline Morrison - approached the stand in turn. Armed with a clipboard and pen they asked their questions and noted our responses. To be fair, it wasn't that dissimilar to the process that we went through in Sheffield. But as individuals we still had to be careful with the answers we gave. The questions may have been similar but they were not the same. Each 'Smiler' had to remain focussed and alert throughout the interviewing phase. Mistakes at this point could cost us the competition. As the judges completed their set of questions they were each presented with a KH Smilers, specially designed and planted, commemorative pot. Bedecked in a fine dark suit, white collar and tie Mr Doolan then expertly delivered the plants to the judge's tables. Interflora eat your heart out!

Everything stopped for lunch at 1.00pm. This provided a welcome break from the pressure of having to answer one detailed and probing question after another. It also gave us the chance to take stock and assess our performance. Overall, we were reasonably happy that everyone had done their best and that we still had a good chance of winning something. However, it was not quite over. Whilst we had our buffet the judges were also meeting to compare notes. The result of this would be a final interview with them all at about 1.45pm. The five of us made our way to the Parlour a few minutes before we were due in. It was like waiting to be called in to a dentist's surgery. Butterflies were not only fluttering in my stomach, they were also doing the occasional back flip. For some reason I was more nervous about this session than anything previously. At last we were called in. Those pesky flutterbyes disappeared instantly, and I was ready for the fray. Fifteen minutes later it was all over. We had answered all of the judges' supplementary questions honestly and to the best of our ability. The team couldn't have done any more. Now, for today at least, it was all over. It was time to go back to the Strand Palace and relax before the Gala Dinner (chomp! chomp! you're going to like this one) at 8.00pm. Also at the dinner would be Vic and Mr Doolan.

We spent the next few hours in our hotel flitting from room to room. As long as the five of us we were back at the Savoy by 6.40pm the time was ours to fritter away as we wanted. So we listened to music, watched the TV, made the odd hot drink, chatted endlessly about our experiences to date, and on a couple of occasions even speculated about what tomorrow might bring. Eventually, it was time to get ready for the Gala Dinner. As usual we all scrubbed up well. Unfortunately, once again Richard was forced to miss out. No matter how we tried we just couldn't get

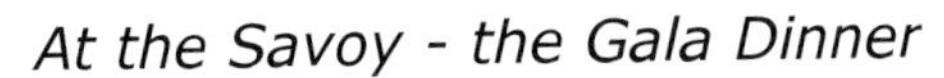
At the Savoy - the Gala Dinner

him a ticket. He was left to spend the evening with the rest of the party – Julie, Tony, my mum and the Grimsta. Not much consolation there I know, but it was the best that we could offer.

By the time people began to arrive at 7.00pm we had already been at our trade stand for ten minutes. As soon as the guests had helped themselves to a drink they set off on the grand tour. Twelve trade stands in forty five minutes. It was a busy time for both guests and teams. However, the one guest that we were all especially keen to meet was Martin Johnson. As captain of England, in the year that they won the Rugby Union World Cup, this man was a celebrity in every sense of the word. Suddenly he was there. What a shock. Standing right in front of us his huge frame seemed to block out all the light. I craned my neck backwards to catch a glimpse of his face. To be tackled by him, I mused to myself, must be like being hit by a double-decker bus. At that point we exchanged a few words, he shook my hand and moved on. I was then gripped by my second shock of the evening. The man had the biggest hands that I had ever seen. To say that they were the size of dinner plates would be an understatement. The thought of being gripped by either of those huge paws sent a shiver down my spine. I made a mental note never to upset him.

Just before 8.00pm guests and achievers began to leave the Lincoln Room to make their way to the Ballroom for the celebration dinner. Being the Savoy you can imagine what it must have been like. The room was large and elegant. The tables were beautifully and sumptuously laid out. The whiteness of the tablecloths and napkins was blinding. The silver cutlery and crystal cut glasses gleamed and sparkled in the light of the candles that had been lit on each table. The diners formally and richly dressed. It was truly a wondrous sight to behold. I had certainly never seen anything like it before, not even at the Cutler's Hall. I was determined to live the experience to the full. Another chance like this would probably never come my way again.

When everyone had been seated, Michael Geoghegan (Chairman, Young Enterprise UK and Chief Executive, HSBC Bank plc) welcomed us all to the event, and introduced a pre-recorded message from George Brown. As the then Chancellor of the Exchequer, he was full of praise for what we had all achieved. Then Martin Johnson took to the stage and recalled the hard work and mental discipline that went into winning the World Cup. He acknowledged the massive impact a piece of individual brilliance could have in a game like rugby, but he was absolutely convinced that the value of good team work and a good team spirit should never be underestimated. One could not flourish without the other. He held this to be equally true in the world of business and enterprise. As he continued with this analogy I found myself agreeing with everything he said, and by the time his speech was drawing to an end, I felt well and truly inspired. He received a thunderous round of applause for his efforts. It was well deserved.

For this particular event the 'Smilers' had been split up. I was on a table with Mike, Kathryn, Vic, Peter Jeffs and several other sponsors and supporters of Young Enterprise UK. Although we had all enjoyed Martin Johnson's speech we were now looking forward to the food (snarl!) The menu was another culinary delight. (But don't worry - my protective clothing is all in place). The starter was a wonderful terrine of melted Beaufort cheese with new potatoes and marinated salmon. This was followed by a mouth watering loin of Welsh lamb with a fine herbs crust, dauphinoise potatoes, green haricot beans and baby carrots. The dessert was an exquisite sticky toffee and apple pudding with vanilla ice cream. Savoy blend coffee and steaming pralines brought the whole meal to a fitting conclusion. A fine dining experience, if ever there was one.

The After Dinner Speakers, Adam Cox (YE past student and

Director of Radio Relations) and Caroline Morrison (MD of Beartas, YE Company of the Year 2003) were both interesting and entertaining. Their YE experiences had certainly been of help to them. Finally, two presentations were made. First, the YE Business Adviser of the Year Award and second, the YE ICT Award. Now, there was only one thing left to do. Track down Martin Johnson and get his autograph. However, as you might expect I was not alone in my quest. Eventually, we all managed to get our programmes signed (I still can't get over those hands) and we left the Savoy for the Strand Palace.

As we walked down The Strand towards our hotel the cool night air was remarkably refreshing. It couldn't have been far off 11.00pm. Flanked by Vic, Janet Brumby and Mr Doolan we arrived at the hotel, went through the lobby and into the bar area where the rest of our party was waiting. Everyone was eager to hear about the Celebration Dinner. It was then that I noticed some new additions to the KH Smilers Supporters Club. Mike's dad and one of Mike's younger brothers had arrived in town and were staying with relatives. Tony Lynn (MFI) was also there. Apparently he had travelled down with Janet earlier in the day. We continued to chat and exchange information for another hour or so, before succumbing to the calls of the Sandman.

Managing Director Dave Garbera, slept peacefully that night. There were definitely no dreams. Well, maybe that's not quite the truth. Gordon Brown may have popped in, but it was only very briefly.

The Day of Judgement

THE day that we had all been waiting for had finally dawned. Back in Hull Stu's parents and my dad were already boarding a train for London. Mr & Mrs Hill were also on their way but by road. They would be the final members of the Supporters Club to join us. It was Tuesday 13 July 2004.

In the hotel everyone seemed to be up earlier than usual. Somewhat subdued we all met up for breakfast. I don't suppose that anyone was particularly hungry, but we thought we ought to eat something, if only to settle our stomachs. Then it was back to our rooms to get changed. Although we had worn our suits on the day before, the whole team was willing to make an extra special effort to look even smarter and more professional. We wanted to look and feel the part more than ever. As a result, we gave our shoes an extra shine, we made sure that our shirts were spotless, we meticulously checked our suits for any stray bits of fluff and made a supreme effort to tie our ties with the crispest of knots. Then, in turn, each of us took a step back and surveyed our handiwork in the mirror. We looked fantastic. Not a hair was out of place. Badges were perfectly positioned. Our confidence was sky high. We left the Strand Palace that morning to a chorus of goodwill messages. It was just before 8.00am. At one point, as we walked boldly and purposefully towards the Savoy, the five of us stretched across the footpath in a line. Now, imagine that scene in slow motion. It was like a clip from a modern gangster movie. We felt and looked unbeatable.

Once again the 'Smilers' entered the Savoy through the River Entrance, but on this occasion there was one big difference. Richard was with us. Although he would not be involved in the Company Presentation, he would be allowed to man the trade stand with us when the guests arrived later in the morning. For the first time we were all together, and a team again.

At 8.15am all the teams were called into the Ballroom for a final briefing and seating rehearsal. We also practised the 'run-in'. This would be how the twelve teams would enter the Ballroom to begin the final round of Company Presentations. On cue, sixty of us would simply jog in to the darkened room and head for our allotted seats.

Back in the Lincoln Room, the six of us prepared the trade stand for the final time. The laptop was set up, the plants were checked and watered and the all important bowl of sweets was filled up for the last time. Down the centre of the room the Savoy staff had covered the judges' tables with clean, white tablecloths, and laid out, in very neat rows, all the paraphernalia necessary for our guests to help themselves to a cup of tea or coffee. However, before guests were allowed in to view the displays, Kathryn and I positioned ourselves either side of the entrance doors. With stickers and flyers in hand we presented everyone who entered the room with both. In no time at all, scores of yellow KH Smilers stickers could be seen all around the room. Having said that, one or two were discarded as quickly as they had been given. For example, one of our rivals from another team was most indignant when her mother turned up at her trade stand apparently supporting another team - KH Smilers. Well, we thought it was funny even if she didn't. But by this time my dad had arrived, so I spent some time telling him about our experiences over the last couple of days. The team also took the opportunity to have a chat with Peter Jeffs, who would be introducing us to the four hundred people in the audience. There was also just enough time for us to complete one final run through of the Company Presentation.

Not long after 10.30am the Lincoln Room was empty. All the guests and judges had been called into the Ballroom. Just the twelve teams remained. We got ourselves in line and waited for the cue. The run-in was only minutes away. You could have cut the tension in the room with a knife. Nerves were clearly frayed and jangling. Locked in our own thoughts and fears everybody fell silent. As I took a couple of deep breaths and tried to relax there was no more time for composure, someone gave the signal and we were off.

Led out by Blink and Pink Zebra we entered the Ballroom at pace from the right hand side. As we made our way along the front, the audience were on their feet clapping and cheering. KH Smilers were towards the end of the line sandwiched between Rag Bags and S.O.S. First was Richard, followed by Benn, Mike, Kathryn, Stu and myself. Slightly breathless but wholly elated we took our seats. We would be the second team to present.

My heart was thumping noisily in my chest as Peter Jeffs (Chief Executive YE Yorkshire & Humber) took to the stage. In just a few moments time we would be up there ourselves. Four hundred pairs of eyes focused on us. Four hundred pairs of ears listening to what we had to say. It was no wonder that I was feeling somewhat apprehensive. But despite these random thoughts and emotions I managed to keep tabs on Peter's speech. "The Yorkshire & Humber finalists this year are a six strong team from Year 10 – fifteen year olds – from Kelvin Hall Secondary School in Hull. That to start with ticks all the Learning and Skills Councils hot spots.........These youngsters have proved themselves an equal match to older and perhaps wiser – who knows? – Company

Programme achievers, as well as the established and mature traders. Ladies and gentlemen, representing Yorkshire & Humber, can you please welcome KH Smilers". We were on. To the sounds of clapping, some cheering (probably our parents at the back of the room) and the theme tune from Ground Force we marched onto the stage. Stu and I moved across to the right, whilst Kathryn and Mike stayed on the left. For the next five minutes we would be the centre of attention, and hopefully, we wouldn't let ourselves, our school or the mighty city of Hull down in the process. At last the performance could begin.

DAVE

Good morning, ladies and gentlemen and welcome to the KH Smilers company presentation. I'm Dave Garbera, Managing Director, and you will be meeting the rest of the team shortly. We are all in Year 10 at Kelvin Hall School in Hull. This presentation aims to give you a potted history of our company, and perhaps most importantly, to show how the team members have grown and developed along the way – just like our plants! Although our school was keen for us to take part in Young Enterprise, it does not offer Business Studies as a GCSE option, so we had a lot to learn. Initially, we bought in a range of mail order novelty gifts but the sales were disastrous. By Christmas 2003 we had a mountain of stock with no sales on the horizon, £250 of unpaid invoices and only two of the original team members remaining.

In January immediate action had to be taken for KH Smilers to survive. An EGM was called which resulted in a new board of directors and a brand new company image. With no time to lose, we discussed ideas for products and finally after a lot of 'trowel and error' we dug up the idea of bedding plants! This was instantly popular among the group and we quickly began to market the project.

STU

Our marketing campaign included a range of themed posters, leaflets, flyers and business cards. As the IT director, it was my responsibility to create and maintain a company web site. I incorporated a staff message board which greatly aided communication. We introduced a company logo and catchy slogan - 'Growing a Smile'. Both are used on our trade stand, company newsletters, and all promotional literature. We have also designed a number of PowerPoint presentations to help promote the business.

MIKE

Determined not to make the same mistake again we took orders in advance of purchasing seeds and plug plants to ascertain the level of demand. At last our business was blooming, and we agreed to set ourselves some challenging, yet realistic, sales targets. A lot of effort was put into this, and I am delighted to report that our initial target of 3000 spring sowings has now been met.

KATHRYN

One of KH Smilers most memorable events was Venturefest York 2004. This was our first real opportunity to promote our company outside of the local area. We learned many new skills on the day – including how to work together in an organised way and more importantly - how to network! We have featured in the Hull Daily Mail and the Business section on regular occasions. The team has also been 'adopted' by The Hull Wednesday chapter of Business Network International who invite us on a regular basis to their 7am breakfast meetings.

Following our success in the Humber finals, the Lord Mayor of Hull invited us to a civic reception, where we were honoured to make history by being the first young people to enter the council chambers and take part in a full council meeting.

MIKE

Over the past few months our Finance director, Richard Myers and other team members have improved their knowledge of bookkeeping by using a Sage accounting program. Recently we have implemented internet banking, which makes checking the bank balance more of a pleasure, now that it is thriving at £1360, ensuring a healthy dividend for our brave shareholders!

DAVE

As you can see from the screen, all of our plants are grown organically in three greenhouses. Between the team, we check the plants daily but most of the spade work is done at the weekends. (STU Which sadly meant no Sunday lie – ins for the team!). Operations Director Benn Jessney is responsible for quality control. This includes checking for any unhealthy plants that might cause disease. To keep our plants healthy, we use organic methods and strictly prohibit the use of pesticides. I am very pleased to tell you, that all our plants are happy in their new homes!

STU

So – what does the future hold for KH Smilers? We will be diversifying our products with the changing seasons until 31st July when, sadly, our Young Enterprise year draws to an end. Until then, we are planning to create a range of hanging baskets and plant arrangements. We have also recently been asked to supply table decorations for a Gala Dinner at the prestigious KC stadium in Hull.

DAVE

This year has been an unforgettable experience for us all, and we have enjoyed working together immensely. Not only have we learned how to run a successful business, but we also succeeded in turning our company round when it had hit rock bottom. Valuable skills for our future careers have also been developed. Things like loyalty, respect for other people's opinions, taking a risk and being responsible for the outcome are all prime examples and it is these things that make us very proud to be here today.

Finally, I hope that we have given you a flavour of the fortunes of KH Smilers since its creation in September of 2003 and we will continue to keep on 'Growing a Smile'! On behalf of the entire team I would like to say thank you for watching our presentation. Thank you.

We left the stage to the sound of clapping, cheering (probably parents again) and the Ground Force music. Seamless and faultless, this was the most professional performance that we had ever given. More importantly, we hadn't let anyone down. Heads held high and totally full of ourselves we returned to our seats and sat down. After such an 'adrenalin rush' of an experience we could hardly contain our excitement. This audience had seen us at our very best. The only difficult part was going to be watching another ten teams go through their paces. But to be fair, every company produced a great performance. It was going to be very difficult for the judges to pick the best three out of this lot. However, if I was totally honest I didn't care which three, as long as KH Smilers was

Final day at the Savoy

one of them. Two YE Founder's Awards for individual achievement completed the first half of the programme.

Lunch in the Lincoln Room came and went. It was nice to have a short break, but as you can imagine our minds were just on one thing. So no matter how much we chatted and paced around the room, the final result was always uppermost in our thoughts. Not even the wonderful food made any difference. We just wanted, no, we needed, to know which of the twelve, was the best YE Company in the UK. I can't speak for the rest, but patience was never one of my strong points.

At about 1.30pm people began to move back into the Ballroom. Once seated, the lights dimmed and John Rendall took to the stage. As well as being the Head of Business Banking for the HSBC he was also, on this occasion, the Chair of the judges. The event recommenced. His feedback on the Savoy competition was very positive. All the teams had done themselves justice and they could take a lot of pride in their achievement. However, inevitably, as in any competition, there had to be an overall winner, but we could all take comfort in the fact that it had been very close, and as a result, the decision to pick the best company had been a very difficult one to make. Unfortunately, we would have to wait a little longer for that announcement to be made. His speech was then followed by the presentation of two awards. First, the YE Marketing Award, supported by Nestle Waters Powwow, and second, the YE Production Award, supported by GKN plc. Disappointingly, KH Smilers featured in neither. The final 'act' before Peter Westgarth announced the top three companies was Nigel Griffiths MP, Minister for Small Business and Enterprise. Like all the speakers at this event, he proved to be amusing, interesting and entertaining in equal measure. But to be honest, by this point, I was only waiting for one thing. Moreover, those butterflies were starting to flutter and my heart rate was beginning to climb. As I scanned the rest of the team for signs of anxiety he finished. The time had come to find out just how good KH Smilers really were.

Peter Westgarth took centre stage and introduced this final phase of the proceedings. After a short preamble the moment had arrived. He was about to reveal the names of the two runners-up and the ultimate winner of the 2004 competition. The six of us took a deep breath as the first announcement was made.

"In third place, winning a cheque for £500 and a commemorative trophy" – the gold envelope was opened and the contents read - "it's Pathways". The audience clapped and cheered as the team jumped up and made their way to the stage to collect their prize. We exhaled. There was still a chance. Peter Westgarth continued.

"In second place, winning a cheque for £750 and a commemorative trophy the winners are" – the second gold envelope was opened – "it's Orkney Ink". Once again clapping and cheering as the team went up onto the stage to get their award. I exchanged nervous glances with the other 'Smilers'. This was it. There were only two options left. We had either won the most coveted prize in the YE Company Programme, or KH Smilers was going home with nothing. I truly believed that it was going to be the former. My life as MD of the company flashed before me. Tension gripped as my breathing became rapid and shallow. I moved to the very edge of the seat. I was ready to go. Peter Westgarth made his last announcement.

"And now the moment we have all been waiting for. In first place, winning a cheque for £1000, a commemorative trophy and for five of the team and their adviser and teacher a visit to No.11 Downing Street this afternoon, and an all expenses paid trip to Malta to represent the UK at the YE Europe Company of the Year competition in just two weeks time. Here it is. In first place" – the final gold envelope was opened and the contents checked - "it's Underwood Visions". An explosion of noise as the whole team and their supporters got to their feet. The Company from Wales was absolutely euphoric. They ran onto the stage, collected the prizes and celebrated their win in front of the whole audience. For KH Smilers it was over. To say that we were devastated would be an understatement. Losing was a totally unique experience for us. We had always won. Maybe it was our age, maybe we were a little emotionally immature, but we found it very difficult to believe that we would be going back to Hull with the swag bag empty. We were just not equipped for failure, and for at least one of the team that meant shedding a few tears in private.

We met up with our parents, Vic, Janet Brumby, Tony Lynn and Mr Doolan in the Lincoln Room at about 3.00pm. As expected they were also disappointed that we hadn't made the top three, but they were far more positive about the whole YE experience, especially the last few days at the Savoy. That was fine for them, but for us I thought it was just too early after the event to be so detached. We needed some time to process what had happened and then we would be able to move on. At that moment we were beyond consolation. Meanwhile we concentrated on dismantling the trade stand. The man in the van would soon be outside the River Entrance. In readiness we took everything out on to the pavement and waited. Not long after the van arrived it was quickly loaded and the driver began his return journey to Hull. He would deliver the contents to the house the following morning. The team returned to the Strand Palace to ponder our loss.

That evening all the achievers went to Maxwell's, an American Bar & Grill, in Covent Garden for a farewell meal. Although we exchanged pleasantries with the members of other teams it was on the whole a rather subdued affair. Most of us had been physically and mentally drained by the events of the past few days and all we wanted to do was to go back to the hotel and get some sleep. Apart from my mum, the Grimsta and Vic, everyone else had returned to Hull.

By 10.30pm Dave Garbera, MD of KH Smilers was in bed and fast asleep. The dream was over.

The next morning Stu returned to the Savoy to attend a meeting of the Saatchi Focus Group. A member from each Company had been asked to return and give their reactions to the whole YE experience. Job done he returned in the early afternoon with 'Chickie Cheques' (KFC vouchers) for the whole team. We then left the hotel and spent the rest of the day doing a bit of sightseeing. Unfortunately, just thirty minutes before we were due to leave London, Mike realised he had left his mobile phone at the Strand Palace. Whilst the rest of us made our way to Kings Cross my mum and Mike made a mad dash to retrieve the missing phone.

Happily it was recovered in time and at 19.33pm we all boarded the train for Hull.

Our date with destiny hadn't turned out quite as planned but no-one could ever accuse us of not having done our best. We had worked our socks off to become the best YE Company in the UK, but it simply wasn't to be. 2004 was the year for Wales and Underwood Visions and not for Hull and KH Smilers. We may have been down but we certainly weren't out, not by a long chalk. KH Smilers returned to the north bank of the Humber ready to move on. The foundations for an even bigger and better KH Smilers were already being laid. In the grand scheme of things losing at the Savoy was only a minor setback!

Going Limited

ON the Thursday morning I got up as usual and went to school. It felt good to get back to normal. But then I was forgetting the Grand Parade. For the last time ever we went into the staffroom. Even though Mr Doolan gave us huge credit for what we had achieved I don't think our hearts were really in it. We accepted the applause of the staff gratefully and returned to our tutor groups. Then, you've guessed it, double Maths. The school, however, hadn't quite finished with us yet.

We returned as Guest Speakers on two separate occasions. On Monday 19 and Wednesday 21 July KH Smilers reprised their Company Presentation (with trophies) at a Year 7 and a Year 9 Celebration of Achievement Evening respectively. This was a totally new experience for us. Yes, we did know the presentation word for word, and yes, we were comfortable delivering it to hundreds of pairs of eyes, but this was different. This one was in front of our peers and we weren't quite sure how we would be received. Thankfully, it all went well.

We also had a very enjoyable lunch with the Hull Rotary Club at the Pearson Park Hotel. Yet another fabulous meal was enjoyed by all, and I was now becoming an expert at the sequence of cutlery. We also managed to pick up an order or two!

At the end of that week Kelvin Hall School broke up for the summer holiday and school could be forgotten until September.

As a big thank you to our parents, supporters and brave shareholders we organised another social evening for Monday 26 July at the Goodfellowship. We had also decided that this would be an ideal opportunity for anyone who hadn't seen our trade stand or Company Presentation to do so. By about 5.45pm we were in our suits and ready to leave the house to put up our trade stand. However, even after everything my mum had done to help us, she had organised one final surprise for the team. At exactly 6.00pm a huge stretch-limo turned up on the drive. Our jaws dropped to the floor as it slowly dawned that it had come for us. We were overjoyed, and straight after the obligatory photographs we were whisked away, taken on a grand tour of Hull and its environs. What a regal experience. An hour later the limo returned us to the pub and surprise, surprise more people and even more photographs.

Eventually we said our goodbyes to the driver and his sleek black limo, and made our way to the function room. Fortunately, some of the parents had already assembled the trade stand and displayed our trophies, which meant that we could begin to socialise and welcome all our guests immediately. Once people had been given a chance to have a drink, examine the trade stand and generally have a decent natter KH Smilers took to the floor. For the very last time ever we reproduced our Company Presentation, and for the very final time ever we were clapped and cheered for doing it. The audience were then treated to a DVD I had put together. There were three tapes of footage that Richard had filmed during the course of the trip to London. I had never made a video before, but I taught myself how to put one together on Windows Movie Maker. Searching for a suitable piece of music was a challenge, but eventually I decided on the New Radicals (You've Got The Music In You) as I felt it was uplifting, rather like our story! It was only meant as a bit of fun but people enjoyed it so much that the DVD was played for a second time. By this time a photographer from the Hull Daily Mail had arrived. He had come to take pictures at the event, but in particular of KH Smilers handing over a cheque for £1300 to the Candlelighters, a charity supporting children with leukaemia. It was accepted on behalf of the Candlelighters by Nicky Straw whose own son, David, had suffered from the illness and who had also been a pupil at Kelvin Hall School. The money represented the profits made by KH Smilers and included the shareholders stake/dividend. They all declined the return of their investment. We were delighted that a charity would benefit from the money that we had raised.

Whilst our guests continued to enjoy themselves, the 'Smilers' prepared for the final event. This would involve me thanking everybody for their support, and then individual team members

KH Smilers handing over a cheque to Nicky Straw

Picture courtesy of Hull Daily Mail

making presentations to those who had contributed most to our cause. Four were actually made – my mum and dad, Vic and Martin. Not long after this the evening came to an end. The trophies were packed away and the trade stand was dismantled. Sadly, it only saw the light of day one more time. Similarly, KH Smilers, the YE Company from Kelvin Hall School came to an end. Although the official date for winding up the company wasn't until a few days later, 31 July 2004, it was effectively dead and buried that night.

But that wasn't the end of the story. In many ways it was just the beginning. The YE phase of KH Smilers may have been over

Real Directors of a real company

Picture courtesy of Hull Daily Mail

but the real business world was still out there, and it was waiting. It was waiting for a group of fifteen year old entrepreneurs from a secondary school in Hull to take it by storm. To prove once and for all that coming from the city of Hull was not a barrier to success, and that business-related training need not be sacrificed at the altar of academic excellence. Admittedly, it was never going to be an easy task but we were determined to show that it could be done. Therefore, during the holidays Benn, Mike, Stu and I decided that the old KH Smilers did indeed have the potential to become a 'proper' business - a business that could successfully compete against the more established traders. After all we already had a significant customer base and a ready market into which we could expand. As well as taking advice from our parents and local business men and women, we used the Internet to research our options. Sadofskys accountants gave us invaluable advice and support. Indeed, as reported in the Hull Daily Mail, KH Smilers always believed in stronger links between the classroom and the workplace (Appendix 5).

By the beginning of October a decision had been made. KH Smilers would be going limited. As well as making good business sense, limited liability would also afford the directors the best possible protection if the company was ever to find itself in severe financial difficulties.

The appropriate forms and support materials were then quickly downloaded from the Companies House website. As we watched the printer spit out page after page after page of information/forms the euphoria at the prospect of becoming real directors of a real company began to ebb away. Before we would be allowed to conquer the world the necessary paperwork would have to be completed. In the end this wasn't as daunting a task as it originally appeared. Time was set aside to read and examine the documentation, and eventually, with care and patience, everything was filled in correctly. We chose to have equal shares in the company. Our investment of £100 each meant that our total liability would be £400. However, I will admit to one thing at this point, a degree in form filling would have been very useful. Bureaucracy! What would we do without it?

Nevertheless, a solicitor was soon found to sign the necessary documents (purchased and downloaded on the Internet), a cheque was written to cover the registration fee and, together with all the other paperwork, the whole lot was sent off to Wales. Just three weeks later I received a large brown envelope through the post. Inside was a certificate from Companies House in Cardiff. As from 29 October 2004 we were Company No. 5273331. KH Smilers had been re-born as KH Smilers Ltd. We were now a proper company with proper directors (us), and officially part of the local business community. And, don't forget, the four of us were still at school, albeit in the final year, with an average age of fifteen. Not bad for a bunch of ordinary kids from a comprehensive school in Hull! We may have lost at the Savoy, but we were determined not to lose in life. As far as we were concerned the spring season couldn't come quickly enough for us to prove it.

"No-one Ever Remembers Who Came Second"

BY the end of February 2005 our seeds had been planted and our plug plants ordered. New staging to increase the capacity of each greenhouse had been bought and fitted in place. Compost and planting trays had arrived. New order forms had been designed, and flyers for our marketing campaign printed and already delivered. The revamped and updated web shop was on-line. KH Smilers Ltd was more than ready for the new season. Even though our GCSE exams were just round the corner, we all felt that with effective time management, we could definitely run the business and pass our exams. From the start, we accepted that difficult situations could arise at certain times during the year, but they would never be impossible to resolve. As long as we planned ahead and shared the work load nothing would be allowed to stand in the way of our success. Results day in August would prove it – one way or the other!

Actually we hadn't been completely idle in the previous six months. Obviously we had our GCSEs to prepare for but we also found time to fulfil a contract for the Hull Junior Chamber of Commerce (September) for table decorations, as well as completing several speaking engagements. In September we addressed a meeting of teachers who were interested in Young Enterprise and the programmes it offered. It was quite funny really, because it wasn't until we were more than halfway to the

Darley's Arms in Hessle that we realised Benn wasn't with us. We had forgotten to pick him up. Doing a u-turn and then battling with early evening traffic to try and stay on time proved to be a bit of a nightmare. However, against all the odds we made it.

In October we did a presentation for the Hull Business Forum to encourage businesses to create more opportunities to work with young people in schools. We met many people from the local business community and found it very surprising that they already knew us and had been following our progress.

Finally, my first solo engagement. In January 2005 I was asked by the Learning & Skills Councll (Humberside), to attend its Staff Training Day at the Royal Hotel in the city centre, to give a talk about my experiences as MD of KH Smilers and of KH Smilers Ltd. I felt very privileged to have been asked and thoroughly enjoyed myself. In fact I was invited to return two months later to take part in a similar event. I must have been good!

Throughout March and April orders for plants and hanging baskets arrived almost daily through the post. Our web shop was doing steady business and we felt it was an excellent sales aid. It took a long time to input all the descriptions of the plants, but was well worth it. The feedback from customers was excellent, as they could learn about the plants before purchasing at their leisure. Telephone orders were also a popular way for our customers to place an order. It was obvious that those long, back breaking hours spent putting order forms and flyers through people's letter boxes in wet and freezing conditions was paying massive dividends. The suffering had clearly been worth it. Our target of growing and selling 12000 plants had been comfortably met. In our very first season as a Limited company we had quadrupled our output and would realise a healthy profit from our investment. This was great news.

Easter was early in 2005. A short family holiday in Edinburgh had been booked a few weeks earlier, and we would be leaving Hull by train early on 25 March, Good Friday. In the meantime we had agreed to landscape Janet Brumby's front garden. On the morning of Thursday 24 March we left Hull early to complete the first phase of the project – digging up and removing all the old shrubs and bushes. [Phase 2 – fitting wooden edging, planting with heathers and in-filling with plum coloured slate – would be completed a week or so later]. Job done we returned home only to find that the Royal Mail had also been busy. In the front porch, neatly stacked, were dozens of boxes containing thousands of plug plants. This was not good news. I was going on holiday the next

Benn, Stu, Mike and Dave hard at work planting

day and they would all have to be replanted in their proper trays. The team were going to have to put in some overtime. The harsh reality of running a real business hit us like a bolt of lightning. It had to be done and we had to do it. Absolutely exhausted, and working under arc lights set up by my dad, the last tray of plants went into the greenhouse at 10.00pm. We had worked virtually non-stop for about twelve hours. KH Smilers Ltd and its quartet of directors learnt a very important planning lesson that day.

On a happier note by the middle of May our 12000 plus plants were developing beautifully and only a week or so away from delivery. We set up a delivery schedule by telephoning customers each evening to inform them their plants would be ready shortly. Nearly a year on, the Hull Daily Mail was also interested in the progress that we had made (Appendix 6).

Revision for the forthcoming exams was also progressing according to plan and it was around this time (12 May), funnily enough the evening before my French Oral Exam, that I fulfilled my engagement as the Keynote speaker at the YE Humber Strategic Final, held at the Tickton Grange Hotel, just outside Beverley. The presentation reflected my experiences as MD of KH Smilers and the progress that the company had made since the Savoy finals in 2004. As I sat down at the end of my speech I was glad that I had been part of this event, but I was more than glad that I wasn't actually competing.

On Monday 6 June, I attended the official launch of the Hull & East Riding Business Week. Then four days later I was given the opportunity to spend the day at the GEMTEC Arena as part of the Yorkshire International Business Convention. Sitting amongst some of the most influential local and regional business people, I was privileged to hear speeches by Archbishop Desmond Tutu and former USA Secretary of State, General Colin Powell.

By mid June all our plants and hanging baskets had been safely delivered. We received many phone calls and letters thanking us for our good service and congratulating us on the quality of the plants.

We also completed a contract for Young Enterprise to supply table decorations for the Regional Finals at the Guildhall in Hull.

Outstanding invoices had been paid and our profits securely under lock and key. A great cause for celebration if ever there was one, except for the fact that the four of us were slap bang in the middle of our GCSE exams. There can be no doubt that this was a very hectic time for us but we all coped well with the pressure. Indeed, I would say we thrived on it, although good self-management did help a great deal.

June drew to an end and so did our exams. We felt that we had worked hard and done enough to achieve all the A* to C grades that we needed. Just a few days after, the four of us walked through the main entrance of the school for the last time and we left Kelvin Hall behind. Eleven years of compulsory education was over. But this was no time for tears. We were already thinking about next year; already thinking about expanding the business.

But running a business at sixteen years of age is incredibly frustrating. For a start being taken seriously was a constant battle and uphill struggle. Obstacles on our path to fame and fortune were great and many. But the greatest of them all..........getting a business bank account. Without a KH Smilers Ltd bank account we could not take advantage of any of the trade deals and discounts that we were offered, and believe me or not, we tried over and over again. But it was always the same. No bank statement in the name of KH Smilers Ltd, no line of credit or discounts available. This was really disappointing and to some extent disheartening. The four of us really wanted to do everything ourselves; we were capable of doing everything ourselves except, you've guessed it, opening a business bank account. Every time we mentioned our age and admitted we were still at school, each bank we visited politely showed us the door. They wouldn't even explore the possibility of opening an account. To us, it just didn't seem to make any sense. After all, it wasn't as if we were actually asking them for anything, we just wanted somewhere to put our hard earned money and get a statement. We couldn't believe that bank after bank didn't want to take our money. Whatever next? A global financial crisis and banks going bust!

However, we did not give up. To a large degree it made us even more determined to get what we needed. Eventually, the breakthrough that we were hoping for finally arrived. The Business Department of one bank was prepared to consider us, Lloyds TSB. Their representative, Frank Cullis, listened to us carefully, examined our business plan, checked our identities (we took our passports) and took our individual details. He promised to pass it on to his superior who would make the final decision. A week or so later we got the answer we were hoping for, but with one proviso, a responsible adult over the age of eighteen would have to countersign the agreement. Without this token adult, there could be no way forward. We didn't really want that kind of involvement, but if we wanted the bank account we had no choice. My dad was over 18, and responsible for most of the time, so we took him with us to sign the agreement. At last, KH Smilers Ltd had a business bank account, and on 26 August we made our first hefty deposit.

Once we had our first bank statement we set about applying for trade cards. KH Smilers Ltd could now obtain credit and take advantage of any discounts available. However, signing up for a trade card at B&Q proved particularly amusing. From the start the person we spoke to was extremely sceptical. Four young lads wanting to apply for a trade card just didn't feel right. I am sure he thought it was some kind of prank. But, just in case, he gave us the benefit of the doubt and one by one we gave him our personal details – name, address, age and so on. He was clearly unhappy with the fact that we were only 16 years of age. Notwithstanding his continually raised eyebrows, we gritted our teeth and persevered. Eventually he asked for the company name. Very clearly I said "KH Smilers Ltd". Well, his face was a picture. "KH Smilers" he repeated back at me. The grin on his face said it all. If he had been sceptical about our intentions before, now he was absolutely sure that we were pulling his leg. Thankfully, before he had the time to injure himself or us, I passed him the bank statement. As his eyes soaked up the details and his brain processed the information his face slowly returned to its normal colour. As his body relaxed so did his manner. The paperwork was then quickly completed and KH Smilers Ltd left the premises with four temporary cards. We had obtained our first line of credit.

Round about the same time we approached the John Cracknell Youth Enterprise Bank for a grant. It had been specifically set up with the purpose of giving young people in Hull the financial support they might need to make their ideas happen. In our case if KH Smilers Ltd wanted to expand production in 2006 we needed a larger growing capacity. We had the space but not the funding. With lots of encouragement from Charles Cracknell the four of us put a bid together. After doing a vast amount of research we decided that a poly tunnel would be far more cost effective than a greenhouse. As a result we subsequently applied for a grant of £500. Within a short period of time the cheque arrived and a 10ft X 20ft poly tunnel was purchased. This increased our growing capacity by a further 10,000 to 12,000 plants. With the help of the Youth Enterprise Bank we had the potential to double our production in 2006 to 24,000 plants.

There was also the small matter of our GCSE results. The day

The new poly tunnel

came and went. We needn't have worried. All did very well. Between us we had a sack full of GCSEs. The academic and the vocational were now truly walking hand in hand. 'Smilers' were living proof that it was possible to run a successful company at fifteen years of age, and at the same time gain good examination results.

In September we started our A levels at Wyke Sixth Form College. Between the three of us, we were taking thirteen A level courses! At first, it did cross our minds as to whether it would actually be possible to run a business at the same time. There was only one way to find out. After a few weeks, our minds were put at ease as we fell in to a rhythm, balancing our college work, with KH Smilers. Feeling confident that we could carry on with the business effectively, we began to organise the summer season.

Initially, 'Smilers' was unheard of among staff at the college. We were about to change all that, by telling just about anybody we could! Soon, there was interest from staff and we received orders for bedding plants. Also, the Biology department purchased a number of geraniums to be used in various experiments.

It felt like people were beginning to take the company seriously. We were now older, and hopefully more experienced, with a growing reputation for providing quality products.

On Friday 18 November we supplied living table decorations for the Women of Achievement Awards, held at the Ramada Jarvis Hotel in Willerby. This was a most prestigious occasion, hosted by Jennie Bond the broadcaster and journalist. We delivered the plants in the morning, but as it was an all-ladies event we weren't invited to attend!

The company had also entered the Hull Daily Mail Business Awards in the Start-Up Business of the Year category (Appendix 7), and had recently completed a short promotional video to be shown at the event. We were also featured in the Hull Daily Mail on at least two occasions that month. KH Smilers Ltd had been chosen as one of the three finalists. Hosted by Harry Gration (broadcaster and rugby league fanatic), the Awards evening was held at the KC Stadium on Thursday 24 November 2005. This black tie 'do' began with a champagne reception at 7.00pm and was followed by a lip-smacking four course meal (growl!). First, roast plum tomato soup served with fresh coriander & a continental bread basket. Second, three types of salmon served with a lemon crème fraiche & mixed leaves. Third, oven roasted chicken filled with wild mushrooms in a light white wine and sage sauce served with seasonal vegetables. Fourth, mango & passion fruit

Picture courtesy of Hull Daily Mail

Hull Daily Mail Business Awards

delice with a passion fruit syrup. I ask you, is it any wonder that I get through so many bibs? Unfortunately, 'Smilers' didn't win in our nominated category, but we were presented with a certificate, and it felt good to be rubbing shoulders with some of the most important business people in the Hull area. It was worth every penny!

January 2006 brought a return trip to the Ramada Jarvis Hotel for a meeting of the Hull Business Forum where Mike and I did a short presentation bringing them up-to-date with our progress. We also became official members of the group that evening.

A week later we delivered order forms to our established customers. In order to increase sales we targeted new areas into which the company could expand. Each weekend, we delivered letters and flyers. Although time consuming, it was a very cost effective way of marketing our business and products.

It was also time to assemble Poly our 20ft long poly tunnel. It quickly became apparent that a degree in structural engineering might have been useful. However, after a couple of days' hard work she was up. The most beautiful polythene clad structure I had ever seen. She was now ready, willing and able to nurture our precious plants and hanging baskets.

KH Smilers was also featured in a Hull Daily Mail article celebrating YE's decision to become a Cityimage bondholder, a scheme designed to promote the city of Hull (Appendix 8).

By early April the majority of orders were in and we had virtually sold all of our stocks of plants. We were also pleased to see a significant rise in the number of hanging baskets that had been ordered. This increased our profitability and was, therefore, very welcome.

Two months later it was all over for another summer season. Well, not quite. All of the greenhouses and poly tunnel had to be cleaned out and disinfected. I must admit, this is not one of my favourite jobs but you have to take the rough with the smooth!

Due to our success KH Smilers Ltd had further exposure in the Hull Daily Mail (Appendix 9)

On 18 May, I attended the YE Humber Celebration & Awards Evening to present the Communications prize. This was held at the KC Stadium and the occasion brought a lot of good memories flooding back. I was just thankful it wasn't KH Smilers that was competing anymore.

A couple of weeks later KH Smilers Ltd set up its YE Company Programme trade stand for the very last time. It was taken out of storage for the 10th Hull and Humber Chamber of Commerce Expo 2006. A hugely enjoyable event, we spent the time networking and selling. Pleasure and profit. What more could you ask for?

It was also at this point that Stu decided to resign from the company. With all of his other commitments he felt unable to give KH Smilers Ltd the time it deserved. This was a sad loss but a loss

From eighteen to three

that the company could survive. We took stock and moved on.

Sometime in August the three of us were discussing the 2007 season when we realised two things. Firstly we hadn't yet tapped into the winter market for bedding plants, and second if we were going to expand production again we would need to buy another greenhouse.

The first decision was easy, although we did realise we were taking a risk by venturing into the winter market. We had not grown these types of plants before. We would grow 5000 winter bedding plants and simply market them amongst our existing customers. We felt that this was a realistic target for our first season in this market.

The second decision would involve more finance. The company

needed a loan. A bid of £750 was, therefore, put together and sent to the Youth Enterprise Bank. They did not let us down. Later in the year a cheque for the full amount was received and banked.

By the beginning of September my dad had completed his great escape from teaching. This made him very happy. He had also won a Radio Humberside pen for answering the lyrics question on the Andy Comfort Breakfast Show. It was something to do with Peter Gabriel and the song 'Biko'. No, I'd never heard of it either! That's probably why he won – neither had anyone else. Initially we were all very pleased, but after a few weeks of him constantly asking us if we wanted to borrow his 'Andy Comfort Radio Humberside' pen, we were heartily sick of it. There was a plan to kidnap the pen, but he guarded it at all times. It even went to bed with him! And before you ask, the answer is 'yes', my dad still has the pen. Slightly more worrying, however, is that he is now beginning to see THE pen as some sort of family heirloom, and is threatening to leave it to me in his will. How sad is that?

On the other hand, our winter bedding plants were behaving rather more normally. Pansy, Viola, Polyanthus and Primrose had all been planted and were well on the way. Customers were informed and there was a steady stream of orders. We sold our entire stock. Six weeks later the greenhouses were once more silent and empty and needed cleaning yet again.

During October KH Smilers was approached by Jon Los, a local entrepreneur and Director of Vista, a garden centre on the outskirts of Beverley. The centre had opened earlier in the year with the express intention of sourcing as many products as possible from the local region. He was also keen for small local companies to trade from his premises. As there was plenty of glasshouse space on the site already he wanted to explore the possibility of KH Smilers Ltd relocating to Vista. We were just the sort of company he was looking for - local, vibrant and prepared to take a risk. This would be a huge opportunity for the business to expand both its range of products and its market share. It was a very exciting development for us and totally supported our belief that KH Smilers was having a real and significant impact in the local area. Unfortunately, before any concrete plans could be made Vista was sold and the opportunity disappeared. And so did our dreams of becoming millionaires by the time we were 21. Never mind. Que sera sera. Applying for university places was also high on our agenda.

As the year drew to an end a new website designed to help teenagers start their own businesses came on line. In partnership with Yorkshire Forward the Young People's Enterprise Forum had launched the Wildfire website. It was aimed at 14 to 18 year olds who could register to create their own business homepages, and access expert advice to develop their business ideas. They would also be able to read about the experiences of other entrepreneurs such as Coffee Republic founder, Sahar Hashemi. After being guided through online tasks, site members would receive a copy of their business plan to show potential investors. They would also be given advice on how to find business support via Business Link. I was particularly pleased to be involved with this project, as I believed that I could readily identify with the problems faced by any young person trying to start up their own business (Appendix 10).

In early 2007 our fourth greenhouse was bought and erected. We also invested in five 4 tier Growhouses. Combined with our existing growing capacity this meant that we could increase production to about 32000 plants in the summer. By now we were offering free delivery in the Hull area, and a refill service for our customers' existing hanging baskets. Both proved very popular, especially in attracting new business. Our range of plants was also increased. The web shop was totally revamped making it much more user friendly, and new areas were targeted for leafleting. Another season had begun.

February brought a nice surprise in the form of a very, very glossy publication. Produced by Phil Haskins of PFH Productions, 'Welcome To Hull. Introductory Guide 2007', mentioned KH Smilers in the section on Education and Skills. We were more than pleased to receive our acknowledgement in the same paragraph as that of Michelle Dewberry, famous for winning TVs 'The Apprentice' and ex-pupil of Sydney Smith High School, Hull. Or should it be the other way round? Maybe Michelle Dewberry should be the one pleased to be mentioned in the same paragraph as KH Smilers. I'll let you be the judge of that one.

Just before it was time to start delivering our plants in May, Penny Perry from Young Enterprise Alumni arrived with a film crew to spend the day making a film about KH Smilers. We had been selected to be a case study as we were valued members of the alumni. Over the years, several alumni have set up their own companies as a result of taking part in the competition. It is very unusual for a business which was formed during the competition to continue and flourish. KH Smilers was an exception. The DVD would be shown at the Savoy YE Company Programme later in the year and then distributed to schools nationally. We had made videos before but this was proper film making with a director, soundman, cameraman and lighting. The only thing that was missing was make up. But Benn and I didn't need that kind of help anyway. We were good looking enough as it was!

Plant deliveries started in late May, and for the first time we didn't need any help with the driving, as I had passed my test in February. By mid June it was all over. As usual we had sold out of bedding plants, but for the first time the company had filled nearly 100 hanging baskets and containers, including two very large raised beds at Wyke. It had been another good season and we were now in a position to repay the £750 loan from the Youth Enterprise Bank.

Thursday 16 August, however, would be a particularly important day for the three of us. On that day the results of our hard work over the past two years would be finally revealed. The A-Level results would be out. For the second time, our achievements would show whether or not it was possible to run a successful company and study for academic excellence at the same time. Early that morning, with yet another film maker in tow, we had the proof. As trembling hands opened up the envelopes, and our eyes feasted on the results it was smiles all round for the 'Smilers'. University places had been secured. Moreover, the

Below & right: Raised beds at Wyke Sixth Form College

evidence was crystal clear. Careers in academia and business were not mutually exclusive. In fact I would go as far as to say we benefitted enormously from this partnership. Four years on, the business and its directors were blooming. I was also interviewed by KCFM that morning. My individual results were one of the best in the College (Appendix 11).

The film maker who was with us on results day was from Stream, Hull's own, on-demand, broadband television service. He had been shooting a video about KH Smilers Ltd. From September onwards it would be available for anyone interested in Hull to access. The Stream website promoted and supported Hull businesses. In fact this was our second video for this organisation. We had done something similar the previous year that was eventually shown at The Deep (Hull's own submarium) as part of an event hosted by the Hull ICT Alliance, promoting the use of IT in business.

September arrived and some important decisions had to be made. To some degree they were forced upon us, because in two or three weeks time we would be leaving to start university (Appendix 12). Firstly, the coming winter season. We had time to do the preliminary work, including planting, but no time to complete the aftercare and final delivery. Fortunately, my dad had both the time and the inclination to help us out. Secondly, running the company from three separate university sites. We all wanted to carry on but didn't really know how that could be done. Thankfully, Vic was able to recommend the perfect solution – the Sage 50 Accounts Professional Online Package. It was exactly what we were looking for and it meant that we could share and work with data from multiple locations.

In the spring of 2008 we hit the same problem as we had in the autumn before. But once again my dad was on hand to support us. He agreed to look after our stocks, as well as to start the deliveries for us. Luckily, my course finished in early June, so I was able to get back to Hull and complete the deliveries myself.

The results of a competition for which I had been nominated, arrived just as I returned home. The letter and accompanying glossy booklet were from JA-YE Europe (Junior Achievement – Young Enterprise Europe), thanking me for participating in the Young Entrepreneur of the Year Competition 2008. Even though I hadn't won, I had made it to the final round as one of the best 37 nominees from all over Europe. I was very pleased with this, especially as I was the only one nominated from the UK. I wonder if that makes me the best young entrepreneur in the UK? Probably not.

At the beginning of June, after my end of year exams were over, I received a call from a journalist from the Financial Times. He wanted to interview me for an article which would be printed the following week (Appendix 13). By this time, I was used to giving interviews in person and over the phone. It seemed a little strange on this occasion, though, as I was in the middle of a very crowded Alton Towers! The journalist joked, "It's very noisy where you are, it sounds like you're at a theme park!" How perceptive of him! I was actually in a huge queue for one of the rides. Thankfully, I managed to do the interview before my turn!

Then, another surprise. KH Smilers received an invitation from Young Enterprise UK to attend The HSBC YE Innovation Awards 2008. They wanted us to make one of the after dinner speeches at the Celebration Dinner, to be held in the Park Lane Hotel. We all eagerly agreed. After all we had never stayed in the Park Lane before. And we didn't on this occasion either. Never mind, it gave us the chance to dust off our suits and do a company presentation again. Just like the good old days. The three of us got together the night before and worked on our speech. We practised it over and over again so that we were word perfect. On stage it looks so much more professional than reading from cards. I couldn't wait!

Benn, Mike and I travelled down to London on Tuesday 15 July. We checked into the Premier Inn inside the former County Hall, and spent the remainder of the day having some lunch, darting in and out of shops and even doing some site seeing. Late in the afternoon we returned to change into our suits, and then made our way to the Park Lane Hotel. The process was bringing back a lot of memories, and funnily enough a few butterflies. We met up with Penny Perry at about 6.00pm for a quick rehearsal. At 8.00pm Michael Geoghegan CBE, welcomed everyone to the dinner and then Andy Powell (CEO, Edge) gave a short speech. Together with Helen Wooldridge (Cuddledry Ltd), KH Smilers was presented with the YE Alumni Award. This was awarded in recognition of exceptional achievements and contributions to the work of YE by alumni members. We were all very honoured to accept this accolade. Then came the moment the three of us had been waiting for. Our chance to address the audience. This really was like going back to 2004, but happily, this time, we were part of the entertainment and not part of the competition. As I looked out into that sea of faces, I can distinctly remember being very grateful that our performance that night was not being judged, except, perhaps, by a hungry audience who would rather be eating than listening to us.

Which brings me nicely on to the food (burp!), and for the last time ever, having wrapped myself in reams of Bounty kitchen roll, I shall describe the menu. The starter was a delicious boudin of sole and girolle mushrooms. This was followed by a wonderful crown roasted supreme chicken, pommery mustard sauce, mushrooms and baby onions, caramalised apple and endive. A delightful chocolate and raspberry parfait with raspberry sorbet ended the meal. Marvellous. Sometimes, you know, I think that I should have trained to become a chef. The evening continued with after dinner addresses by Sir Michael Savory (UK Chief Executive, YE) and Jason Robinson OBE (England Rugby International – with normal hands as far as I could see), and concluded with three awards within the YE Company Programme.

The next day we were guests of Young Enterprise at the Awards Ceremony. As we walked into the Park Lane Hotel all the emotions of this day four years ago came tumbling into focus. If the event had been held at the Savoy, I think that the whole experience would have been even more intense than it was already becoming. At that moment in time I knew precisely what every single achiever was going through. Moreover, I knew exactly how the majority would be feeling at the end of the event. That was something I was not looking forward to. There was, however, one consolation. The 'Smilers' speech from the previous evening had clearly demonstrated that the dream did not have to end at the same time as the competition. Yes, it was difficult to accept that we hadn't won, but the skills that we had worked so hard to acquire in the process didn't suddenly cease to become useful overnight. We continued to use them and develop them, and as a result had stood before them as directors of a thriving company, and successful undergraduates. We were all extremely proud of that. KH Smilers returned home the same day.

The following morning, I promised myself a long lay in, as I was tired from the exertion of the last couple of days. This wasn't to be! I received a call at 9am from a member of the marketing team at Sage UK. The woman wanted to interview me for a case study which they wanted to use as promotional material for the Sage 50 Accounts Professional Online program. I was delighted to be approached as this was fabulous publicity for us. I was asked to email a recent photograph of the directors, but unfortunately, we did not have any which were current. My dad, who luckily also happens to be a keen photographer, took some photographs of the three of us in the garden with our home-grown plants. It took all afternoon, as we had to keep running back inside because of showers. Michelle from Sage emailed me a number of drafts, and we soon agreed on a final version. It was a quick and easy process using email. The two page case study was ready in a matter of days and was uploaded to the Sage website.

In September I returned to Liverpool where, to my surprise, the KH Smilers success story was picked up by the national press. Courtesy of YE Alumni, a journalist from the Guardian rang and said she would like to do an article on me. The interview lasted one and a half hours over the phone. This has happened before with other interviews but then when the article has been published I only receive a one line mention! I expected this to be the same but was really surprised when I read the article in the Guardian and I had nearly a full page with three photographs (Appendix 14). True celebrity status at last. For the greenhouse that is! A week later, the Mail on Sunday featured KH Smilers (Appendix 15). Both stories gave the business and its directors fantastic national exposure. And don't forget this was four years on from our humble YE days. The KH Smilers business model was clearly still working.

On a more personal level, it made me feel good about coming from Hull. After all the bad press that the city has received over the years this was positive and wholly refreshing. KH Smilers has proved that good things do come out of Hull, we just need to shout about them more and make people listen. Hopefully, this book will have the opportunity to do some of that shouting.

But, far more importantly, as far as my dad was concerned anyway, the story was picked up by Radio Humberside. It wanted to feature KH Smilers in the 7.50am business slot on the Andy Comfort Breakfast Show. But if that wasn't enough, the station wanted my dad to be live in the studio whilst I would be available via a telephone link. DJ hero and local admirer would be brought together for a second time.

On Monday 15 September my dad was up bright and early. He wanted to make sure that he wasn't late for his few minutes of fame. At exactly ten minutes to eight we were being broadcast live on Radio Humberside. I think we both enjoyed the interview immensely, but my dad especially so. After all, he had just spent ten minutes with the very man that had been waking him up every morning for years. However, as I talked to him afterwards, over the telephone, I detected a hint of disappointment in his voice. I suspected what it might be, but I didn't say anything. Our conversation continued. Eventually he couldn't help himself and he confessed. My dad had failed to meet his other hero at Radio Humberside; Sunderland supporter, fan of Shakin' Stevens and Andy Comfort's comic foil, the irrepressible Traffic Master himself, Kevin West! I had suspected as much. Fortunately, before my dad could take this failure a stage further, it was time for me to leave for University. Quickly passing on my commiserations I said goodbye and hung up. However, I'm sure he'll get another opportunity in the future. Only time will tell!

Finally, as 2008 came to an end KH Smilers Ltd had been nominated for an award as the European Young Entrepreneur 2008, in the Internet magazine BusinessWeek.com Appendix 16). As one of seventeen finalists we were the only company to be nominated from the UK. The winner to be decided by a European wide public vote. But don't worry, if we win, I'll make sure that you hear about it.

In 2009 we will be featured in the internet magazine 'Inspire', which can be found on the U-Xplore website. This is a site dedicated to providing interactive, reality based careers information, advice and guidance. Through 360° virtual tours of real businesses the site aims to show young people "the good, the bad and the ugly" in the world of work. But that is only the tip of the iceberg. It allows a variety of users to do much, much more than that. It's worth you exploring.

"So, what does the future hold for KH Smilers?" Those were the words uttered by Stu towards the end of our Company Presentations. Well, it wasn't oblivion, that's for sure. We didn't come second, not even third in 2004, but five years on KH Smilers is still here. Still being talked about. Still selling the same product five years on. Older? Yes. Wiser? Probably. But forgotten, no. Most definitely, no! So, to the person who publicly claimed that "no-one ever remembers who came second", I beg to differ. It's how you react to a setback that matters and not the setback itself. KH Smilers, with its Hull born and LEA educated Board of Directors, has proved that many times over.

The Final Word

IT'S another gloomy autumn day in Liverpool. An ideal opportunity for me to complete the company accounts for 2008. As I wait for Sage to load, I gaze out of my rain spattered windows onto Alderson Road. Passers-by, wrapped up against the elements, go about their daily lives. I am glad to be watching them from the warmth and comfort of my ground floor room. My cup of tea is getting cold so I take a sip, turn back to the screen and tap in my password. The program stirs into action. I enter the final few sales, and reconcile the bank. Bingo! It matches the bank statement. Next stop the post box at the top of the street and Andy Jewitt's desk at Sadofskys, active supporter of KH Smilers since our early days at Hull BNI, and now our chartered accountant. The end of another record breaking year is here. We have grown and sold nearly 50000 plants, as well as filling 150 hanging baskets and containers. The business and its directors have come a long way in five years.

Looking back, it is absolutely clear that the experience of running our own company has changed the three of us forever, but it was our involvement in the YE Company Programme that started the ball rolling. Without it, six hardworking, but quiet and unassuming fourteen year olds, from a comprehensive school in Hull, might never have come out of their shells. Might never have been able to stand up with absolute confidence, and do a presentation in front of four hundred people at the Savoy Hotel. Furthermore, without the support and advice from the local business community, especially Vic at GCS, we would never have had the opportunity to learn, and then put into practice, the skills that have helped us to run KH Smilers so successfully. Moreover, these are exactly the same skills that we used, and are still using to be successful in our academic lives. They are truly transferable. The directors of KH Smilers have proved, beyond a shadow of a doubt, that the worlds of business and academia are not mutually exclusive. It doesn't have to be an 'either/or' choice. With commitment, hard work and a positive attitude they can be moulded into a great partnership.

Having said all that, I must also acknowledge the huge impact that the use of modern technology has had on KH Smilers. From its power to attract new customers to its ability to maximise the efficient running of a business, the use of IT can never be underestimated. Without the power to run our business remotely, everything would be twice as hard to do. Fortunately, we all learned the skills to manipulate this technology at school and at GCS. They have been invaluable to say the least.

Many years ago an old man once said to me, "David, hitch your wagon to a star". Having traced the hugely successful development of KH Smilers and my career alongside it, I can honestly say, that for the first time, I think that I understand what he meant. He was obviously a lot wiser than I gave him credit for at the time.

Well, I must go now. I don't want to be late. Tonight there's going to be a full moon, and I'll be dining out in Liverpool somewhere. Bon appétit!

APPENDICES

Appendix 1

"Enterprising pupils blossom in business"

Hull Daily Mail – 9 March 2004

An ambitious team of young entrepreneurs have won the backing from local businesses in their bid to claim the Young Enterprise crown.

The Young Enterprise scheme allows teams of pupils from secondary schools to establish their own business and run it as part of their studies.

Successful businesses can win their way through a regional competition to take part in a national contest to find the best business.

Teams have to establish their own company, raise share capital, and appoint people to senior positions in accounts, marketing and business development.

And the dedicated team behind the KH Smilers business at Kelvin Hall School, Hull, have sought the backing of some of the region's firms to get them off to the best possible start.

George Street-based Golding Computer Services has already offered its support with IT, accounts and business planning advice.

It also has used its links to bring accountancy giant Sage on board, which has supplied an accountancy package.

Now, the five strong team is planning to visit a meeting of Hull's Business Networking International (BNI), in a bid to gain more commercial support.

Managing director Dave Garbera said he was confident the business would be a success.

It has already secured orders in the region of £400, and is now looking to build its customer base by attending a range of business networking events.

He said: "We attended the Venturefest event in York and that was very useful for us. We are confident that we can be successful with this business.

"At the end of the day, Young Enterprise businesses are not just judged on their profitability, but the way the business has been handled and run.

"It is also important to get backing from local businesses.

"Whilst they are not able to give us any financial support, they can help us with services and products, and we have already found many to be very supportive of Young Enterprise.

"Hopefully the BNI meeting will give us the opportunity to put our business in front of people who might be able to support us."

Appendix 2

"Students sowing seeds of success"

Hull Daily Mail – 17 May 2004

It could be a model of any modern business – trouble in the boardroom, a profits warning and the constant battle to please shareholders.

But the difference about the KH Smilers is none of them is older than 15 years of age.

And the six-strong team of entrepreneurs have already proved they have what it takes to succeed in the competitive world of commerce by sweeping the board at the Humber region's HSBC Young Enterprise Innovations Awards.

The Smilers, who all attend Kelvin Hall secondary school in Bricknell Avenue, Hull, won five of the seven awards available.

And the title of MFI Winning Company means they go forward to the regional final at the historic Cutler's Hall in Sheffield.

Victory there will see them challenge for the national title in London.

The winner of the national prize will then compete against other countries in the European Company of the Year awards in Valetta, Malta, in July.

These are heady days for a business that only began life last September. What's more, the company nearly went bust in its first weeks of trading.

The then 18 members of staff dedicated themselves to making and selling novelty gifts. But they soon found themselves £250 in debt. Heads rolled, directors resigned and the new streamlined team decided to move into the plant and flower market.

Since then, business has bloomed. With long hours spent in meetings at Kelvin when other pupils had gone home, and the almost nightly vigil in greenhouses across the city, the Smilers are now boasting a £391 profit – much to the delight of their shareholders.

From seed, the firm has planted and organically grown more than 3,000 plants, including geraniums, busy lizzies, petunias and verbena. Most have been ordered through the company's website, at www.khsmilers.co.uk.

"It's been really hard work but very rewarding," said managing director Dave Garbera, 15.

"I'd say the secrets to success are communication and teamwork. We were really poor at that in the beginning but we've worked hard to turn it around.

"The competition itself is something that drives us on, but the other motivation is to try to be a success. We are determined to finish the project, make a profit and to be a success."

He added: "None of us expected it, we were ecstatic when they announced the result."

The business offered shares up to a maximum of £10 and held fundraising events to gather the £80 registration fee to get going.

Now, they have nearly sold all their stock and when this goes they will donate any profit to charity.

ICT director Stu Vernon, 15, said: "If anyone wants to place an order we will try to meet it but we would urge them to be quick as we're nearly out of stock."

Their performance has also brought a smile to the face of their headteacher, Martin Doolan.

He said: "The key thing is they are only in year 10 and they have been up against sixth-form competition.

"For a year 10 team to win against that sort of competition is very impressive and they didn't just win through, they swept the board."

Mr Doolan said he had also noticed a change in their personal development.

He said: "They have become so much more confident and so much more mature. I'm delighted."

Appendix 3

"Enterprising city students mix with region's business leaders"

Hull Daily Mail – 15 June 2004

Among the high-profile figures which filled the venue, a group of city students intermingled and shared their thoughts on business in Hull and the East Riding.

Young enterprise students from Kelvin Hall School were awarded for their outstanding success this year with tickets to the big event.

And the KH Smilers team, who have collected nine awards this year are now preparing for the Yorkshire and Humber finals, picked up some great tips on the day.

However, the group were split up on arrival and sent to different tables representing various industries across Hull and the East Riding.

And they soon found themselves sitting with some of the region's most influential figures.

It was a day Kathryn Hill, 15, Richard Myers, 14 and Dave Garbera, 15, are unlikely to forget in a hurry.

They were even tracked down by one of the speakers, Tim Sanders, chief solutions officers of Internet giant, Yahoo, who was keen to hear about their work.

He has even asked the three Hull students to remain in contact and keep him updated with how their business is progressing.

Dave, managing director of the Young Enterprise business, said: "The whole day was extremely enjoyable, and it was great for us to hear such inspirational speakers as we prepare for the finals of our competition.

"The Young Enterprise scheme has given us so much more confidence over the past 12 months, and the speakers on the day showed just how important it is to have belief in yourself."

While television impressionist Rory Bremner won the vote for the most enjoyable speech, Dave and his team were also heavily impressed with both Tim Sanders and Miles Hilton-Barber.

Former Conservative leader William Hague surprised the students with a speech full of one-liners.

Dave added: "I expected William Hague to be quite drab, but he was very funny and entertaining.

"I am sure that we will all benefit from having attended and met many influential people."

Janet Brumby, development manager for Young Enterprise in the Hull and East Riding region, said it had been a "once in a lifetime" opportunity for the students.

She said: "I am delighted that they have been rewarded for their hard work in such a marvellous way."

Appendix 4

"Contest plants business seed"

Hull Daily Mail – June 2004

A Group of budding business leaders aim to be crowned national young enterprise champions.

Pupils from Kelvin Hall secondary school, Bricknell Avenue, Hull, have just won the regional heat of the Young Enterprise competition.

Now year 10 students Kathryn Hill, Michael Jones, Richard Myers, David Garbera, Benn Jessney and Stu Vernon will travel to London to pit their enterprise skills against the best students in the country.

The pupils formed a company called KH Smilers and cultivated bedding plants.

Richard, 14, finance director, said: "It's amazing. I still can't believe it.

"It was a great experience to be up against the best teams from the region."

If the team wins at the event in The Savoy in London on July 13, it will secure a £1,000 prize and a trip to Malta.

The six teenagers sold 3,000 bedding plants grown in greenhouses belonging to 15-year-old managing director David's parents.

They made £1,650, of which they will donate £650 to children's cancer charity Candlelighters.

After costs and paying back shareholders they will be left with £700.

The competition has given the six teenagers a sense of direction. Stu Vernon, IT director, said: "I'm planning to go into business now.

"Before I hadn't even thought of that option."

Kelvin Hall headteacher Martin Doolan said: "They are super students anyway but the increase in their confidence and their personal growth since they started this company has been remarkable."

The team members are younger than their competition but do not consider it an issue.

Richard said: "It doesn't change anything. We know we are as good, otherwise we wouldn't be where we are."

Stu attributed the company's success to communication and organisation.

He said: "At first we found it hard to balance studying for our exams and keeping the company going, but we learnt to manage our time properly."

The company started with an 18-member board.

But when they made a £250 loss on novelty toys, only Richard and Stu decided to continue, and they were joined by four others.

Next year, the group plan to produce hanging baskets.

Appendix 5

"Give us a link with firms"

Hull Daily Mail – 27 October 2004

A group of classroom entrepreneurs hailed as the best young business executives in Yorkshire today urged schools to forge closer partnerships with industry.

The call came after a survey of Hull businesses said almost nine out of 10 companies felt school-leavers were not up to the jobs they applied for.

The survey, for the Hull Business Forum, found:

- *Eighty-eight per cent of businesses said the quality of young people currently entering work did not meet their needs for new employees.*
- *Ninety-one per cent of firms believe attitude is more important than qualifications.*
- *Thirty-five per cent believe attitudes in young people are getting worse, while 14 per cent believe they are improving.*

But Dave Garbera, managing director of Young Enterprise team KH Smilers, said: "I don't think attitudes are getting worse, but there should be more opportunities for businesses to work with schools, because you need a balance between academic and business skills."

The Smilers and a team from Hymers College gave presentations to the forum on Monday.

City council education director Helen McMullen told the forum the city's GCSE results were improving, but not quickly enough.

Forum manager Nick Pontone, said: "We understand results are improving but businesses want to see an acceleration in the city's progress."

The KH Smilers, formed at Kelvin Hall High School in Bricknell Avenue, west Hull, won the regional finals of the Young Enterprise scheme, which sees pupils establish and run their own businesses, in the summer.

The firm produces and sells bedding plants.

Appendix 6

"Sowing seeds of business success"

Hull Daily Mail – 10 May 2005

Bedding business minds are proving they are the cream of the crop.

Just one year ago, four 15-year-old Kelvin Hall School pupils set about creating their own plant business.

And they proved such a success that they were crowned Yorkshire and Humber winners of the Young enterprise event last year.

The pupils from the Bricknell Avenue School in west Hull, developed their idea of growing bedding plants from seed to sell locally.

But instead of winding up the company as originally intended, the determined quartet of managing directors, Dave Garbera, Benn Jessney, Stu Vernon and Michael Jones, decided they would take things to the next level.

They took their first tentative steps into the real world of business with rookie company KH Smilers in November.

And from producing just 3,000 bedding plants for the Young Enterprise Project, they have just shifted more than 12,000 plants they have grown in greenhouses at their homes.

Dave Garbera said: "We had our work cut out to make a success of the business. We had a lot of learning to do.

"We had to learn how to sow and care for beddings plants, how to design and plant hanging baskets and table decorations."

The boys contacted a computer software company in Newcastle, which gave them a copy of its accounting programmes.

Dave said: "It is amazing how fame opens doors for you. After winning the Young Enterprise event we found ourselves giving talks and speeches to many organisations.

"We felt that we had taken the company too far to abandon it. We owed it to our plants to continue.

"After discussions with our parents and business adviser, we realised it would be possible to combine our school studies with running a fully operational limited company.

"We are now experts in form-filling, business meetings and the art of persuasion.

"It is very difficult to be taken seriously at 15 and 16 years of age."

The company has already completed a contract for the junior chamber of commerce and grown and sold more than 12,000 plants.

Appendix 7

"We just can't stop our school project growing"

Hull Daily Mail – 9 November 2005

Four teenagers have taken a project they started at school under the Young Enterprise scheme into the real world.

KH Smilers has been so successful, it is now a finalist for the Business Link Humber-sponsored Start Up Business Of The Year award at the Mail's Business Awards.

In the company's early stages, it had a mountain of stock, no orders and a £200 debt.

But the former students at Kelvin Hall School in west Hull have transformed the company.

This year, its turnover has topped £2,500 with 61 per cent profit.

KH Smilers supplies organically-grown bedding plant packs, hanging baskets and table decorations to houses, shops, organisations such as the Junior Chamber of Commerce, Humber EBLO and Young Enterprise events, and events including the Women Of Achievement Awards 2005.

It has carved out a niche market among elderly residents who appreciate the free delivery and personal service provided by the four 16-year-olds, who are now studying for A-levels at Wyke Sixth Form College in West Hull.

"Having won the Hull and Humber finals of the Young Enterprise Competition and gone on to the national finals, we decided the business had a viable future," said managing director, David Garbera.

"We decided to continue it and incorporated KH Smilers as a limited company last October.

"This year we've quadrupled our production level to 12,000 plants and expect to double it again next year.

"We plan to buy another greenhouse with a grant from Cracknell Youth Enterprise Bank."

Vic Golding, managing director of Hull's Golding Computer Services, taught the team at weekends about profit and loss, cash flow, stock control and marketing.

The company has a new web shop for orders at www.khsmilers.co.uk, which has already had more than 32,000 hits, and, having just acquired a third-of-an-acre plot, is set for further growth.

Appendix 8

"Youngsters will be great ambassadors for the city"

Hull Daily Mail – 1 March 2006

Young Enterprise has helped produce some of Hull's finest young ambassadors.

Now the organisation is itself becoming an ambassador for Hull by joining Cityimage's bondholder scheme.

Bondholders sign up to support Cityimage's work promoting Hull as a vibrant and successful place to live, work and invest in.

Hull's successful Young Enterprise companies have in recent years helped promote the region throughout the UK and the world.

Avian Enterprise, the company made up of sixth-formers from Hymers School that produced a range of wooden bird feeders, won the UK Young Enterprise final last year.

The company then won a silver medal at the European final in Oslo.

In 2004, a team of pupils from Kelvin Hall School in west Hull won the competition's Yorkshire and Humber final and also represented Hull at the national final.

The company KH Smilers, which supplied bedding plant packs, hanging baskets and table decorations, was so successful, its pupils decided to continue after leaving school.

Appendix 9

"Firm keeps on growing"

Hull Daily Mail – 13 March 2006

Everything's coming up roses for a group of Hull sixth-form students who set up their own gardening company.

KH Smilers was founded in 2004 as a Young Enterprise company at Kelvin Hall school in west Hull and kept going after its directors moved on to sixth-form college.

The company has now launched its own website and is offering a free delivery service.

Since the start of the year it has almost doubled its production of plants and hanging baskets.

The company's four directors, Stu Vernon, Benn Jessney, Dave Garbera and Michael Jones are now studying at Wyke College and they say business is blooming.

Dave, 17, said: "The website has made a huge difference to the business.

"We've had a lot more orders on the Internet this time – probably four times more compared with last year."

At Kelvin Hall the firm soon won customers for its range of bedding plants and in 2004 was voted the best Young Enterprise company in Yorkshire, reaching the national final.

When the directors moved on to Wyke College they decided to continue the company.

It was an immediate success, reaching the final of the Mail's Business Awards last year.

David has passed his driving test and is using his new skills to offer a free delivery service to the Smilers' customers.

He said: "That has proved popular because a lot of people prefer their plants to be delivered to them rather than having to pick them up.

"It's particularly popular with elderly people."

The directors plan to keep KH Smilers running themselves until they leave for university in about two years.

David says while his fellow directors are thinking about heading into business, he is looking to move into medicine. But he said: "If the right opportunity came up in business I wouldn't say no."

Vic Golding, managing director of Golding Computer Services, was KH Smilers' business adviser in its Young Enterprise days and still works closely with the company.

He says the team has made successful use of technology, including their website and Sage accounting software, to build their business.

He said: "They're very determined, really prepared and they don't take no for an answer."

Appendix 10

"Wildfire spreads great advice to teenage traders"

Hull Daily Mail – 7 November 2006

A young Hull entrepreneur is backing a new website designed to help teenagers start their own businesses.

Yorkshire Forward has teamed up with the Young People's Enterprise Forum to launch the Wildfire website, providing free, expert advice to youngsters who want to follow their business dreams.

The site is being backed by Dave Garbera, managing director of Hull's KH Smilers, which grew from a Young Enterprise team into a thriving business.

The new website is aimed at 14 to 18-year-olds, who can register to create their own business homepages and access expert advice to develop their business ideas.

They will also be able to read about the experience of other entrepreneurs such as Coffee Republic founder Sahar Hashemi, who addressed the Yorkshire International Business Convention in Hull in 2005.

After being guided through the online tasks, site members will receive a copy of their business plan to show potential investors.

They will also be given advice on how to find business support via Business Link.

Dave Garbera said: "Starting my own business has been an extremely rewarding experience, which has provided me, and my colleagues, with valuable business skills such as teamwork, communication and leadership.

"The Wildfire programme is excellent for young entrepreneurs and I am delighted to be involved as I can readily identify with the situations young people starting in business are faced with today."

KH Smilers, which produces bedding plants, hanging baskets and decorative arrangements, was founded in 2003 as a Young Enterprise company at west Hull's Kelvin Hall School.

The company made the national final of the Young Enterprise competition before its directors decided to "go it alone" and continue the business as a limited company.

Appendix 11

"David sows the seeds of Uni success"

Hull Daily Mail – 21 August 2007

David Garbera is no stranger to success.

The 18-year-old Wyke College student is managing director of KH Smilers, a Young Enterprise company he started with friends while at Kelvin Hall School.

The company, founded in 2004, sells bedding plants grown from seed and won the regional finals of the Young Enterprise scheme that year.

Now David is celebrating four A grades in A-level biology, chemistry, English language and general studies and a B in physics.

He will now study medicine at Liverpool University.

He said: "I was definitely nervous before I opened my results.

"Before I picked them up, I had checked on the UCAS website to see if I had got into my first choice and I had so I am really pleased.

"The results are better than I hoped for. I was worried about physics, but got a B."

Appendix 12

"Smiles over our growing firm"

Hull Daily Mail – 28 August 2007

It started as a school project by a group of ambitious teenagers.

Now, almost four years on, KH Smilers' horticultural business is still thriving.

The former Young Enterprise firm this year grew 35,000 plants and produced more than 100 hanging baskets and planters.

Its three remaining directors now plan to use the profits from the business to help fund their way through university.

Managing director, Dave Garbera, 18, of west Hull, said: "I was surprised how well we have done.

"We've got an established customer base. It has been a good learning curve."

KH Smilers was founded by about 20 pupils from Kelvin Hall School in north Hull.

It went on to become one of Hull's most successful Young Enterprise teams.

It won the Yorkshire and Humber title in 2004, making it through to the national final.

KH Smilers grew 3,000 bedding plants in its first year.

Instead of winding up the company as originally intended, the firm's directors registered it as a limited company and continued to trade.

Mr Garbera said: "We joined KH Smilers soon after it was formed. It started off with about 20 people making Christmas cards.

"Others dropped out because they did not realise what was involved and we decided to turn it round to the

bedding plants idea.

"None of us were particularly horticulturally-minded, but we have learned a lot through doing it.

"Young Enterprise has taught us about working as a team and communicating with each other and customers.

"It gave us a sense of what it's like to run a business."

KH Smilers grows flowers and shrubs in greenhouses and polytubes in Mr Garbera's parents' garden.

It now intends to grow 50,000 plants by the winter. This year they expect to make a £3,500 profit, making a total of more than £8,000 profit.

Mr Garbera, sales director Mike Jones and operations director Benn Jessney have just completed A-Levels at Wyke College in west Hull.

They intend to continue the business while at university. Mr Garbera said: "At certain times of the year it is quite a lot of work.

"My dad, Andy, will maintain the plants when we are away.

Appendix 13

"Schools spur on start-ups "

The Financial Times – June 2008

Studying a course in enterprise at school gives youngsters more confidence to start a business, writes Jonathan Moules.

An education charity is claiming proof that entrepreneurship can be taught to young people after a survey found that its alumni were twice as likely as their peers to be involved in start-ups.

A six-month study of about 2,000 people by the Freshminds consultancy found that 14 per cent of those who had completed the Young Enterprise Company Programme at school went on to create a business, compared with 7 per cent of those who had been on the course.

Among those aged 18 to 21, the difference was even more stark, with 16 per cent of the Young Enterprise alumni setting up their own compared with 3 per cent for those who had not.

The findings add weight to the idea that entrepreneurship can be taught, rather than being something a person is born to do.

Young Enterprise graduate Dave Garbera started KH Smilers, the bedding plants retailer, with two friends while studying for his GCSEs, and has continued running the business while studying to be a doctor.

"Before Young Enterprise my perception was that business was boring," he said, adding that the profits from KH Smilers is helping to pay his way through university.

"Medicine is still my number one priority, but I would like to keep the business running as long as possible," he said.

Appendix 14

"The next big thing"

The Guardian - 6 September 2008

Medical student David Garbera is one of thousands of undergraduates who developed business skills thanks to a Young Enterprise programme at school. What's remarkable about Garbera is that he's still running his Young Enterprise project with his friends Mike Jones and Ben Jessney. Called KH Smilers, it's a bedding plant business, which enjoys a healthy turnover and has won 15 awards.

Among the accolades was a third-place position in the Start-Up Business of the Year category in the Hull Daily Mail Business Awards of 2005. The trio, all 16 at the time, beat scores of established local businesses to get so far in the competition.

Garbera describes the night their victory was announced, at a lavish black-tie ceremony, as "exciting". The awards inspired the friends to continue the business and, three years on, it's a profitable limited company.

"KH Smilers has been growing every year since its launch," says Garbera. "Last year we used the profit from the business to buy ourselves laptops for university."

The friends had a busy summer with the business, selling bedding plants they grew in January from seeds and plug plants. "We sell roughly 50,000 bedding plants a year and over 100 hanging baskets. Because the business is seasonal, it doesn't interrupt our studies."

KH Smilers was initially born out of adversity at Kelvin Hall school in Hull, back in December 2003, after the founders of a novelty gifts business - which Garbera and his friends had just joined - decided to quit the venture.

Garbera, Jones and Jessney were left with debts of £250. Determined to clear them, they brainstormed and soon decided that the best way forwards was to set up a plant business.

"We weren't into plants but we tried to think of the resources available to us," recalls Garbera. "I had two greenhouses in my back garden and a lot of people buy bedding plants in January, and as it was December we decided to set up a plant business."

Garbera is back at university, having started the second year of his degree. "I'm looking forward to getting into the course," he says. "We will be spending two days a week on the wards at Aintree University Hospital in Liverpool from mid-September onwards, taking blood or giving injections."

In five years' time Garbera hopes to be working as a junior doctor, before specialising in radiology or pathology. But he also hopes that his plant business will still be going strong.

"My dad, who has taken early retirement from teaching, has been helping out and so when we graduate he will be happy to run the business."

Appendix 15

"We're budding teenage tycoons"

The Mail on Sunday – 14 September 2008

Dave Garbera, Mike Jones and Benn Jessney should leave university a little less in debt than most students.

The 19 year-olds are still running KH Smilers, the bedding plants business they set up in 2004 when they were classmates at Kelvin Hall School in Hull.

"Last year we sold 3,000 plants, this year it has been 50,000 and we have turned over about £10,000," says Dave, a medical student at Liverpool University.

Dave, Mike, studying computer science at Leeds University, and Benn, studying medicine at Hull University, set up KH Smilers with help from Young Enterprise, an Oxford-based charity that educates pupils about business and enterprise.

Dave says: "There was no way we would have come up with the idea without them."

But though vocational diplomas, which combine work-based training with classroom study, were launched in schools this month, experts say not enough is being done to foster an entrepreneurial spirit among pupils.

Appendix 16

"Trio in line for top business award"

Hull Daily Mail – 3 December 2008

They set up their own business when they were still in school - and now three Hull entrepreneurs are in line for a major business award.

The three businessmen from KH Smilers have become the youngest nominees in a prestigious competition and the only UK entry to reach the final voting stage of Business Week magazine's annual European Young Entrepreneur contest.

Dave Garbera, 20, Michael Jones, 19 and Benn Jessney, 19, set up KH Smilers in 2004 while they were pupils at Kelvin Hall High School in Bricknell Avenue, west Hull.

Helped by investment from enterprise partnerships, they set about producing a range of naturally-grown bedding plants.

Now their table decorations are first choice for corporate events all over the country and this year they expect to grow 50,000 bedding plants, compared to 3,000 in 2004.

Managing director Dave said they were "honoured" to be representing Hull and the UK in the competition.

He said: "My biggest challenges in setting up the company were lack of business knowledge, funds and, of course, my age.

"It was very difficult to be taken seriously at 15 years old.

"I would suggest to anyone starting up a business to conduct as much market research as possible and enlist the services of Hull's Youth Enterprise partnership.

"The support we received was invaluable."

Councillor Christine Randall, lead member for children and young people's services at Hull City Council, said: "I am so pleased to see our young entrepreneurs up for this award.

"They are a great credit to our city, having gone from being secondary school pupils to university undergraduates and still running the business they set up while on the Young Enterprise Company Programme in 2004.

"They are planning to buy another greenhouse that could allow them to grow tens of thousands of extra plants, proving that sometimes the best business plans are the simplest."

Maureen Foers OBE, chair of the Hull Youth Enterprise Partnership, said: "To succeed in business, you don't have to invent a flashy new product or design the latest gadget.

"For the founders of KH Smilers, it was a business selling plants and hanging baskets in Hull, focusing on top-quality horticultural products that its clients want to buy."

For the next month, people across Europe are invited to read the stories of the young entrepreneurs and vote for the company they think shows the most promise.

To vote for KH Smilers, visit www.businessweek.com and follow the links.

MORE TO COME

Look out for Smilers II: Made in Hull.

In this second of the trilogy I will offer more detailed information and explanations of my own personal journey from 14 to 19, concentrating on how I managed the practical demands of being an entrepreneur with the academic needs of being a full time student.